Breath of India

4 Friends on a Spiritual Pilgrimage

Breath of India

4 Friends on a Spiritual Pilgrimage

Elizabeth Owens

Pisces Publishing
Cassadaga, FL

COPYRIGHT © Breath of India, Elizabeth Owens, 2010

All rights reserved. No part of this book may be used or reproduced in any form whatsoever, including, but not limited to, Internet usage, without written permission from the author, except for a reviewer who may quote brief passages in a critical article/review.

Cover and back cover design by Elizabeth Owens
Photography by Elizabeth Owens

Most of the quotes before each chapter were taken from the book, **The Secret Knowledge**; *Insight into the Spiritual Life,* by Shri Satpal Ji Maharaj. This book may be purchased online at www.manavdharam.com

PISCES PUBLISHING
P.O. Box 55, Cassadaga, FL 32706

Printed in the United States

ISBN 1453616128

9.95

This book is dedicated to my dear soul brothers:

Tim Williams
Dr. James Thomas
Albert Bassett

Table of Contents

Foreword

One:	**The Journey Begins**	**1**
Two:	**Welcome to Delhi!**	**7**
Three:	**The Ashram Experience**	**21**
Four:	**Happy Birthday!**	**40**
Five	**On the Road Again**	**58**
Six:	**Satsang**	**72**
Seven:	**I'm Home, Now What?**	**77**
Eight:	**Shri Vibhu Ji Is Here!**	**85**
	Acknowledgements	**93**

APPENDIX

Packing for India	**94**
Glossary	**97**

FOREWORD

The spiritual experiences written about in this book took place at Prem Nagar Ashram in Haridwar, India. Haridwar is known as the Gateway to Heaven and Prem Nagar is called the City of Love. Resting at the foothills of the Himalayas, Haridwar is one of the holiest pilgrimage destinations in India. For thousands of years, it has been the chosen retreat of saints, sages and pilgrims who, after retiring from worldly pursuits, sought a life of study, meditation and simplicity.

Prem Nagar Ashram is located on the banks of the Ganges River, which is considered a very spiritual body of water. It was the loving creation of Satguru Shri Hans Ji Maharaj, who was in the lineage of perfect Masters who revealed Spiritual Knowledge to their disciples. Founded in 1944, Prem Nagar Ashram was his and his devotees' labor of love. The dream came to fruition over the years with construction beginning in 1950. Devotees leveled the land and constructed a hut where Satguru Shri Hans Ji Maharaj and a few devotees lived. From this humble beginning, Prem Nagar has grown into a huge and unique ashram with more than 1000 rooms.

After Shri Hans Ji passed away in 1966, his wife, Jagat Janani Shri Mata Ji, continued construction and improvements. Their son, Satguru Satpal Ji Maharaj, today continues the work of his father. Prem Nagar is the largest ashram in Haridwar and the main ashram of Satguru Shri Satpal Ji Maharaj. One distinct difference from this ashram compared to others in Haridwar is that it has a Living Master who oversees the ashram and over 3,000 other ashrams in India and Internationally.

Most other ashrams teach a religious view handed down from a now deceased guru or master. All who have visited Prem Nagar agree that there is a living force within the ashram, that being the God-realized Master, Satguru Shri Satpal Ji Maharaj.

The names within this book have not been changed, nor those of the prominent people within the ashram. Since they are public personalities and so revered, I allowed their true identities to be revealed.

Focusing on the breath is where the journey begins.
Shri Vibhu Ji Maharaj

Chapter One
The Journey Begins

It was four weeks out from my trip to India. I was counting the days until I left for what I believed would be my trip of a lifetime. Ever since my early twenties, I had wanted to go to India for a spiritual pilgrimage. At that time I probably didn't really understand what a spiritual pilgrimage was, but I knew now and I definitely wanted this adventure. As a middle aged woman, I had waited long enough.

One reason I was going was because a part of me wanted to know God, and then there was the other part of me that was in trepidation. In my mind, God is omnipresent, omnipotent and omniscient; present everywhere, all powerful and all knowing. Would it be possible for me, or anyone, to actually experience such a wondrous thing? Was it truly possible for *me* to know God? The very idea of someone saying "I know God" sounds like a person with an ego out of control. I would be skeptical of anyone who made such a claim. But here I was, traveling to India to know God. And that kind of scared me.

In September of 2008, a group of my friends visited a large ashram in Haridwar, India, named Prem Nagar, located next to the Ganges River, the exact place I was bound. They had been invited by the Satguru, Shri Satpal Ji Maharaj, during one of his visits to Florida. While staying at the ashram, they were able to participate, if they chose, in an initiation to learn "Knowledge." At this point in writing, I'm not exactly sure what the term "Knowledge" means, only that I will have the same opportunity. The incredibly beautiful spiritual experiences they all spoke about were something I desired. I wanted Knowledge, whatever that meant.

The impetus for this trip for me started in June of 2009 when Shri Vibhu Ji Maharaj, the son of Satguru Shri Satpal Ji Maharaj, visited the Cassadaga Spiritualist Camp in Cassadaga, Florida. He was scheduled to deliver a sermon, to use lay terms, at the church located within the community. I went to hear him with no anticipation or preconceived ideas. I just wanted to hear him speak. Needless to say, I enjoyed his talk. Shri Vibhu Ji was so charismatic, animated and wise, especially for a young man not even thirty years of age.

It was announced that he would be delivering a satsang later that day and all were invited. Satsang was a term I was familiar with. I knew it to be a spiritual discourse because a former friend of mine had a guru and we would attend satsangs on occasion. After hearing the Sunday talk, I was onboard for the satsang. There was no way I would miss hearing him speak again. The satsang did not disappoint. Again, I was caught up in his web of knowledge, charm and humor. I was mesmerized that he did not even cough, take a drink of water or clear his throat the entire time he spoke, which was about three hours. When questions were asked, he had all the answers. I marveled at how a man so young could be so wise and all-knowing. Even with his accent, I found myself clinging to every syllable, hungry for more food for thought.

Due to the interest, which was evident by the enormous amount of people in attendance at both gatherings, it was announced that another satsang would be offered in two days, this time during the evening. I would shuffle some things around and certainly be in attendance. I couldn't miss hearing this young man, the captor of my spiritual heart.

By the third time I had been privileged to hear Shri Vibhu Ji speak, I was a total devotee. That began my inquiry into all things Indian associated with him. This wasn't just some fly-by-night young man with something to sell, a religion to convert people to or a charlatan, he was the real deal. And I wanted more! No one had ever affected me so profoundly. I felt a shift inside me to something much more peaceful. There was an unmistakable change in me that defied description.

Not long after Shri Vibhu Ji Maharaj blessed all of us with his presence, a movement was under way to travel to India for the two day celebration of Satguru Shri Satpal Ji Maharaj's birthday. Shri Vibhu Ji had personally invited a friend of mine, Tim, to attend and others were welcome as well. Shri Vibhu Ji had stayed at Tim and Liz's house when he was visiting Cassadaga and had become dear friends with them. Tim was definitely going. For thirty-six years, since his initiation into Knowledge, Tim had carried a burning desire to place his feet on Indian soil and visit Prem Nagar. For him, it would be heaven on earth.

I was asked by Tim if I wanted to go. Well, of course, I did! But travel to India? I had only been out of the country once in 1983 when I went to Cancun, Mexico for a honeymoon. India was really far away. And then there was the cost of the airfare. And I had a beauty salon to manage. And I had a husband and live-in mother-in-law to consult. It wasn't whether I wanted to go, it was *could* I go?

I ran the idea by my husband who said it was okay with him. Then I approached my mother-in-law, who was raised in the Depression, which makes her extremely frugal where money is concerned. I imagined her saying it wasn't practical. Much to my surprise, she didn't. She thought this was the trip of a lifetime and I should definitely go. I might never get another chance like this, how could I pass it up? Well, push me over with a feather! If she thought I should go, I was going! I immediately emailed Tim and announced, "I'm going to India!"

As it turned out, only four out of ten people who had expressed interest actually traveled to India in September of 2009. And we were a diverse group! We all knew each other through the Cassadaga Spiritualist Camp. Albert is a large, tall man who has been a yoga instructor for many years and I was also a yoga instructor, so we had something in common. Besides his interest in yoga, Albert seemed to have an insatiable appetite to learn about meditation, mantras, Hindu Gods and spiritual philosophy. He had studied and practiced meditation for years. Going to India was a no brainer for Albert.

Dr. Thomas and I had known each other for many years. Dr. T, as I like to call him, is a retired chiropractor, a teacher of metaphysics, spiritual healer, medium and Spiritualist Minister. I had sat in his classes during the days when I was a student developing my mediumship. India would be another step on his spiritual path.

Tim is a big, teddy-bear-kind-of-a-man with inspiring spiritual energy, which made me like him almost immediately. Our first introduction was when he and his wife, Liz, attended a yoga class I was instructing at my yoga studio. We discovered each other again in Cassadaga about a year and a half later after I had closed the studio.

Tim started his spiritual quest much earlier than I when he ran away from home in upstate New York as a teenager. He began seeking God in communes at various locations. In 1973, at age eighteen, he heard a guru speak, Shri Satpal Ji Maharaj, who was a young man of twenty-five at that time. Tim was so inspired by this guru's message of peace and love that he became initiated. At last, Tim's wish would come true to actually visit his guru in India. We all understood that this trip we were about to venture on was especially meaningful for Tim.

As for me, I am an ordained Spiritualist Minister, medium, psychic artist and author of four spiritual development books. Besides my desire for Knowledge, I was planning to describe the phenomenal experiences we would encounter on our trip to India in my next book. This was, for me, another stone on my path to God.

We all began making our arrangements to travel to India. That meant getting a passport if you didn't have one (I did), a visa for India and, of course, buying the plane tickets. During the four weeks prior to take off, I also did a lot of research about what to anticipate regarding the weather, food, clothing, shopping and dos and don'ts of traveling to India. I discovered there were a few important issues for women to be aware of in particular. One important one was to cover up or risk offending the citizens, not to mention, attracting unwanted male attention. Long skirts, pants and any Indian attire were acceptable. However, it was not acceptable to dress in shorts, even for men, wear sleeveless or low cut tops, or short skirts. A scarf was recommended to cover the head when in a temple. Further details for traveling in India, along with my personal recommendations, are available in the Appendix, Packing for India.

My biggest concern, actually my only concern, was my accommodations since I would be traveling with three men. I had been told that it is common for a number of people to sleep in close proximity. The previous year, true to custom, couples and singles of both genders stayed dormitory style in a large room at the ashram. It was my hope that I would have accommodations with only women. It wasn't important to me whether I knew any of the women or not, I just wanted to spend my nights sleeping with only females and conduct daily toiletry functions in the company of the feminine gender.

Just before we flew to India, a wonderful woman named Helen contacted me via email. She lives in Sydney, Australia, and has been an initiate for thirty-six years. The group that traveled to the ashram the previous year had mentioned how helpful she had been during their visit, so I was familiar with Helen when she introduced herself. She told me that she had arranged for me to stay in a room with her and that the three guys would be in a room together. Hooray! That was wonderful news! My fears were alleviated, as I should have expected they would be.

The only question left was, what was I going to find in India? I wasn't the first person to seek a spiritual pilgrimage to India or want to know God. Why, in the 1960s, all the hippies were bent on traveling to India. Maybe some of the draw was the hashish, I don't know, but they certainly were driven to find their guru. Maybe, for them, it was the escape they sought from their reality. The guru would make it all better for them and they would live happily ever after, or something like that.

I knew one other woman who, along with her husband, frequently traveled to India. She offered a lot of suggestions about what to take on the trip and loaned me two scarves. She has a guru, although he is located in the States, not India. While it was not a foreign concept to me that someone would have a guru, probably ninety-nine percent of the people I know do not have a guru.

Maybe I was deluding myself and the answer wasn't in India. I had always been taught that all the answers are inside. But perhaps this guru was supposed to open the windows to my heart so I could see the answers more clearly inside. I knew one thing for certain, I wanted answers. If a guru of this magnitude could remove my blinders so I could see into the consciousness, if I could find my own answers in the future through meditation, if I could know God---I'm trembling now---then it was well worth a trip to India to acquire that knowledge. My trip of a lifetime.....

So, India, here I come!

Open your eyes to the energy, to the presence of God manifesting His omnipresence, omniscience and omnipotence.
Shri Satpal Ji Maharaj

Chapter Two
Welcome to Delhi!

We flew out of the Orlando Regional Airport on Continental Airlines. The plane was cramped, so we all hoped the one flying us to India would be larger than this one taking us to New Jersey. After all, it was a thirteen hour flight to India, 7,623 miles, so creature comforts would be important. We were not disappointed. The plane was huge, nine seats across and countless rows. Leg space was ample and the seats were wide. An individual video screen was attached to the seat in front of every passenger on which we could play games, watch movies or TV shows and keep track of where we were in the sky at any moment. There was music, too. Continental, what a way to fly!

We were given a choice of Indian vegetarian food or Western food. We all selected the vegetarian fare because vegetarian would be all we ate once at the ashram, so the thought was to start adjusting now. The Prem Nagar Ashram required guests to abstain from meat, even when eating at restaurants outside the ashram, during their stay. And that wasn't all we had to abstain from. We weren't allowed to use tobacco products, recreational drugs or imbibe in alcohol. Married couples were asked to abstain from sexual activity during their stay at the ashram. I didn't see any of these abstentions to be out of line. Besides, I didn't smoke or use drugs anyway, and my husband was in Florida. As for no alcohol, I felt that was appropriate under these circumstances where we were trying to achieve a spiritual high, rather than an artificial one.

We arrived in New Delhi around 10 p.m., Indian time. After presenting our paperwork to officials, we retrieved our luggage with no hassles. Thapa, the man assigned by Maharaj Ji's assistant, Lakshman, to collect us at the airport, introduced himself by waving a sign as we walked through the central exit from the luggage area. The sign said, "Mr. Tim and Party."

Sign at the Delhi Airport

Thapa drove us to our hotel. The neighborhood was a bit questionable, with a car plant directly across the street where some seedy looking people were hanging out. I would find out later they were actually sleeping on the ground.

We didn't know what to expect of our accommodations. In India one can pay a pricey fee to stay in a luxurious hotel or not much cash for a place that is adequate but isn't air conditioned, lacks elevators and is sparse on creature comforts. As we walked into the lobby of Hotel Guatum, several smiling faces greeted us and a garland of flowers was placed around our necks.

The lobby was pleasant to the eyes, but not lavish, although there was plenty of marble throughout the entire building, which is common for India. The price was only $50 per night and included breakfast in the restaurant next door. So far, the hotel was looking pretty good.

I was assigned a room across from Tim and Albert. Dr. T was in a room on the opposite side of the elevator. All of us had double beds, including Tim and Albert. Those two big guys and they had to share a double bed!

My room was quite attractive: tile floors and a nice bathroom with a makeshift bidet. A small fridge was provided with juices, water and soda. There was a television with only one station that spoke English, and a small basket of fruit on the desk. And, of course, it was air conditioned. I was pleased with my room and I felt secure, which was all that really mattered.

Around midnight, we managed to get something for dinner at the restaurant. Given the hour and being tired, we ordered a variety of samplings of Indian foods, such as naan bread, a pastry enclosed spinach item, chutneys and other things I didn't recognize. The food was excellent.

After a good night's sleep, we rose when we felt like it. All four of us eventually gathered down at the restaurant to have our first Indian breakfast. It was here that I was introduced by Albert to Chai Masala tea. Evidently he prepared the tea at home. We would have many cups of this delicious concoction during our stay in India, and no two cups were the same. Some had what we thought was pepper in abundance, while other cups of tea were milder. It turned out the bite we tasted in the tea usually came from ginger, although pepper was common as well.

Breakfast this particular morning, which didn't vary by much any given morning, consisted of your choice of scrambled eggs, cereal, toast, mini-muffins, orange juice, fried potatoes, a bean cake and chapattis. Spicy chutney was enjoyed on top of the bean cake by some of us who didn't mind a little heat in the morning. That would be Albert and me. We consistently were the two who were always up for the challenge of spicy food. Poor Dr. T, during his first meal on the airplane, shoved an entire pepper into his mouth, not recognizing it for what it was. No matter what he did, he could not quell the fire for some time! I don't think that pepper did much for his seventy-something-year-old digestion either.

For our first day in India, we hired a driver through the hotel to drive us to an area on the outskirts of Delhi, two hours away, to visit with an elder gentleman who had contacted Dr. T in the States via email. Apparently Guru Ji, the name we called him because he didn't give us a name, is a well known healer. He calls his work Cosmic Beam Therapy. Since Dr. T is a spiritual healer, he was quite interested in visiting with this person. The drive over gave us an opportunity to experience Indian traffic. If you have never been to India, the only way to describe traffic there is simply, crazy. Expect to be scared.

In India, people drive at full tilt buggy speed, honking through every stop sign, intersection and stoplight. I never saw a speed limit posted on a sign anywhere that we traveled in all of India. It doesn't seem to matter either that the light is red when approaching an intersection, that's merely a suggestion, I guess, because everyone breezed through the stoplights without stopping. Any foreigner would be insane to rent a car when there is such a variety of unique transportation to hire. I guess the word is out because I never saw anyone other than an Indian driving a vehicle.

I used to think that Boston had the worst drivers. Apologies to the people of Boston, but when someone is honking at me to move ahead into four lanes of traffic, two going in the opposite direction, and the stream of traffic is relentless in both directions, I think that person is nuts or needs to take a tranquilizer. Multiply that by ten in India.

Two marked lanes of traffic morph into at least three if not four lanes. No kidding. Everyone is straddling the painted line, looking for a chance to dive into the best position. Then there are those who have already claimed a potentially better position, honking all the way. The motorcycles creep in between the cars and the next thing you know there are four lanes of traffic attempting to cross the intersection. It's insane.

The best traffic jam was four lanes becoming eight at an intersection. No one was moving in any direction and all you could hear was the consistent sound of honking. My reaction was to laugh at the ridiculousness of it all. You have to have a sense of humor when traveling in India.

There were small motorbikes, bicycles, small cars and rickshaws. The rickshaws were really motorbikes with a covered two-seat attachment to the rear of the bike, and they were everywhere. No matter where we were, we saw sari clad women precariously perched sidesaddle on a motorbike behind their male partner, hanging onto his midsection with both arms, as he sped through the streets. At times we would see the female holding a baby, and it wasn't unusual to see an additional child riding in between the handlebars and the body of the man who was driving. Add to this mix the not often seen SUVs, which we traveled in consistently, and the buses, and you have pure mayhem. I noticed that all the SUVs we traveled in had heavy duty bumpers and steel guards riding up the front and back of the vehicles. They were impenetrable. That's why I could laugh at close calls. If I had been in a rickshaw, I don't think so.

It was common for me to be in the backseat, observing motorbikes venturing within inches, and I do mean six inches, if that, of the vehicle I was in. Mirrors were more like three inches from scratching any vehicle's exterior paint. At any time I could have easily high fived or shook the hand of any driver on a motorbike if I had put the window down--they were that close. Often, we nodded at each other. There were many close calls, much to Dr. T's chagrin, as he watched a car aiming for the door he was seated behind.

One positive thing I observed about the drivers in India was that people were more civilized than those in the States. I never saw angry, impatient drivers. There were no road rage incidents, yelling or hand gestures. All the drivers during our trip were serene. Now if they could just stop the incessant honking.....

Wild pigs were running around eating garbage beside the dirt road we were traveling on to get to the residence of the healer. Some of the houses were very nice architecturally and colorful. After bouncing through the dirt road, we finally found the healer's residence, which was two stories with a basement. We later learned that Guru Ji didn't occupy the entire house. His wife chose to use the entirety of the house, but her healer husband stayed mostly in the basement.

Guru Ji's daughter directed us down to the basement where we were greeted by this kind soul. He was seated on a concrete square platform that was about one foot high and approximately eight feet in width on all four sides. We later learned that this was also where he slept at night, on his back, with a brick under his neck as a pillow.

Guru Ji talked with us about how he performs his particular healing. He doesn't require a person to be present, a photograph works just as well for him. Guru Ji concentrates on the individual in question and runs his fingers up and down an invisible spine, working on the chakras. To do this, Guru Ji's fingers are facing each other and his hands are positioned about a foot away from his body as he is seated on the concrete platform. He moves his hands up the invisible spine with his fingers wiggling as he feels the energy associated with a particular area. When his hands sway outward, it means there is an abundance of something present, and when the hands sway inward, it means a diminishing of some sort.

Guru Ji performed a healing for all four of us and did not charge. He never charges, merely asking that the person perform a service for him or someone else. He was a lovely soul, full of animation and sincerity. After enjoying tea and snacks, we returned to New Delhi.

The return trip was just as entertaining as the one coming. We saw the ubiquitous cow relaxing in the center median. Sometimes there would be up to six cows basking in the sun while vehicles whizzed by, honking. Occasionally we would see a cow strolling in a lane of traffic, but everyone veered around the animal, with no mishaps occurring. No one dared injure a cow, no matter how rudely the animal behaved. That simply wasn't done.

We drove by the Lotus Temple in New Delhi. It was suggested by our driver that we might like to tour the temple, so we exited the vehicle and purchased tickets. This is an ancient and sprawling structure, located within a large park area. It was an exhausting undertaking to tour in the heat of the day with the sun mercilessly beating down on us. One building had a five story steeple, which we weren't allowed to enter. Apparently at one time young couples betrothed through an arranged marriage jumped off the steeple in protest, so visitors were now forbidden entry. Our tour guide was very informative and friendly to us Americans. After the tour, we paid him his fee and tipped the man generously.

Albert was attracted to a bearded gentleman seated on the grass wearing a turban. He found out the man was a Sikh and he was more than willing to chat with Albert. We then observed a dog nestled into an open area of the trunk of a tree, protecting her puppies. It's common to see dogs roaming loose, like the cows, with no visible owner. All the dogs we saw appeared underfed, neglected and unloved. One thing that struck me was they all looked so similar, as if they all came from the same litter, whether we were in Agra or Delhi. Long snout, pointed ears positioned high on the head that usually drooped down and a short coat.

Next we visited a pricy emporium with hard charging sales people. That would turn out to be the norm, very zealous sales people were everywhere. At this particular emporium, our driver would receive a commission for any purchases we made.

Tim remained outside for a time, desiring to have a smoke and find a diet Coke. Some boys had set up a stand right outside the emporium. When Tim approached the stand, the boys acted rudely, making silly remarks in Hindi, which he didn't understand. But Tim did understand the body language and attitudes. The boys did not have a diet Coke, only Pepsi. All Tim had in the way of money at the time was an American twenty dollar bill, which was not going to work in this situation.

Tim figured out who the leader was and asked him his name and if he spoke English. The boy replied, Arjuna.

With that small piece of information, Tim reared back into a karate stance and mimicked having a bow and arrow like the original Arjuna would have used during the epic battle as depicted in the Bhagavad Gita. Tim declared, "Oh, Arjuna, you were named by your father and are a warrior, huh?"

All the boys looked at Tim quizzically. Now, having their attention, he told the boys how Native American Indians name their children after the first thing that they see or that comes to mind upon first viewing their babies. Tim told Arjuna that perhaps when his father saw him he saw a warrior. After all the theatrics, Arjuna got up to offer his seat to Tim and brought him a diet Pepsi at no charge, then they visited.

Tim does not know a stranger. He felt camaraderie with these street boys, probably because of having acquired his own fair share of street knowledge from when he ran away from home. At this point, our driver came out to encourage Tim to come inside the emporium. Tim declined for the moment, saying he was having fun with the street boys. After a little while the owner of the shop came outside, dressed in Italian loafers and wearing gold rimmed glasses, to see what the delay was. He arrogantly motioned another boy to give him his seat so he could sit across from Tim to determine why he was sitting there rather than shopping.

The owner introduced himself and asked where Tim was from. Upon learning he was American, he made a statement about what a great country America is because all the children go to school. Motioning toward the street boys, Tim asked the emporium owner if he thought those boys had an education? The owner said they did not go to school. Defending his new street friends, Tim explained that perhaps, while not having a formal education, that if they were able to make it on the streets of Delhi they could make it on the streets of any city in the world, even New York City, as these streets were the toughest he had ever seen.

The owner paused, being a bit stymied by that statement. To make the point clearer, Tim pointed out that the most educated lawyer on Wall Street probably could not make it through the night here in Delhi if dropped off with nothing but his own survival ability. However, these boys could survive with no problem if the situation were reversed. Tim said that the value of their street education should not be dismissed. At that point the owner rose and left. Small smiles were evident on the faces of the street boys and Tim felt very safe with them.

We returned to the hotel, freshened up and met down in the restaurant for dinner. I was hungry! We had just ordered drinks when Lakshman appeared. He was due to pick us up later that evening to take us for a visit to the ashram in Delhi, but here he was, early. It seemed that Shri Satpal Ji Maharaj was now at the ashram and wanted us to come immediately for a private visit. This was a special privilege, so, hungry or not, we left the restaurant and piled into the waiting SUV.

We were told that Maharaj Ji had been at Parliament all day and that he had been appointed as Chairman of the Defense Committee. That sounded like a great position for him to occupy since he has promised to bring peace to the world. Perhaps he can achieve some peace at least for India.

We arrived at the ashram, Shri Hans Satsang Bhavan, which is also the location of the head office for the ashrams all over the world. Approximately one hundred people work here. The buildings inside are surrounded by tall, concrete privacy walls. Guards allowed us entry into the compound.

We entered the ashram building itself by a side entrance and were escorted to an outer waiting area of the office in which Maharaj Ji would receive us. Once we were invited to go into the office, we saw Shri Satpal Ji Maharaj seated, with his wife, Mata Shri Amrita Ji, nearby. We sat on couches and spoke with both of them. I was at a loss for words. I just blathered something about meeting his son in Cassadaga and how impressed I was, hence, here I am. I also complimented Mata Ji's beauty. She really is pretty and must have been drop-dead gorgeous in her youth. Tim and Albert had no problem talking. Dr. T said a few words.

At some point Mata Ji left the room to attend to other business. We were asked if we're hungry and, of course, we were. Maharaj Ji ordered food to be served to us. We were escorted out of the office and back to the waiting room where a wonderful meal was served, consisting of rice, lentil vegetable soup, tofu in sauce, naan bread and pasta with veggies in sauce with cheese chunks. The meal was spicy and delicious.

The four of us returned to the hotel to prepare for our trip the next day via train to Haridwar where Prem Nagar Ashram is located and where the birthday celebration will take place. I attempted to charge my cell phone, but it never did take a charge. Evidently the phone had no clue where I was and never did perform the entire time I was in India. The others also had the same problem.

We gathered for breakfast after Dr. T phoned all of our rooms to wake us up. Dr. T is an early riser, so he phoned me first thereafter since I was the most likely person to come down for breakfast. Albert and Tim sometimes didn't answer the phone. On this particular morning, once we were together, Albert and Tim regaled us with tales of their adventure during the wee hours of the morning.

They had gone to sleep, woke up in the middle of the night and decided to seek out the "underground city." To begin with, there is not an underground city in New Delhi. If there had been one, it would have been in the neighborhood of our hotel, according to their taxi driver. They asked him if there was a disco, and he said no to that also. The cabbie took them on a rickshaw ride around town, going down some seedy side streets that made Albert nervous. Once they returned to the hotel, they sat on the steps outside, observing the night life. And they weren't disappointed.

Pretty soon a guy came waltzing by, looking very weird, dressed in black pants, a long gray shirt, a sparkly tiara on his head and a pink scarf around his neck. He was lovingly holding a puppy in one of his arms, much like anyone would carry a baby. In the other hand he carried a long bamboo stick that he tapped on the street as he walked. One of the security guards at the hotel made a twirling motion with his finger beside his head to indicate to Tim and Albert that the guy was nutty.

Remember, Tim doesn't know a stranger, so he was eager to approach this weird guy and walked out to greet him in the street. At this time of night there isn't any traffic. The guy offered the puppy to Tim, which he declined. Albert, his active imagination in full swing, thinks the guy is a demon. Tim later gave this strange man the title Goddess of Darkness. The "goddess" started dancing in the street, raising the ire of the security guards from the hotel. Albert called out that he has Tim's back. However, Tim described the situation more like Albert was far enough away to be in a safety zone.

One guard yelled out at the Goddess of Darkness, motioning him to be on his way. In response the goddess did a little dance shuffle, mocking the guard, and said, "Go, go." Everyone burst out laughing as the Goddess of Darkness departed. And that was as close as Tim and Albert came to an underground city or disco.

After breakfast we were due to be picked up and taken shopping near the train station. However, our transportation was running late, or, I should say, we were on Indian time. Nothing seems to run in a timely fashion in India. Finally, we all piled into two SUVs, luggage and all, and drove to the train station through horrible traffic. Since there is now a concern if we will make the train on time, there will not be any shopping.

We finally arrived at the station, but my tummy was a little upset, so I thought, I'd better take some Dramamine since I will be jiggling around in a train and I don't want to further provoke the condition. The driver and helpers were all scurrying around in the parking lot, grabbing our luggage and heading for the train. I was waiting on Thapa who had my luggage, but he was talking to someone across the parking lot, so I decided to follow the others.

When I walked through the fence, I turned left and kept walking beside the tracks, looking for everyone. All I saw was a sea of brown faces, and not one was vaguely familiar. As I was growing concerned, Thapa ran up beside me with my luggage. He started looking around at the crowd and evidently he didn't see anyone he knew either, so he called on his cell phone. Thapa got off the phone, turned in the opposite direction and yelled back at me, "Run!"

Oh, my God, I thought, we're going to miss the train! I ran behind him as best I could with my upset stomach, wearing sandals, carrying my smaller bag, the temperature feeling like one hundred degrees and I'm already sweating. We dashed to the opposite side (I should have turned right at the fence) where everyone was waiting anxiously for me. Tim was having a panic attack, telling me he was refusing to leave on the train without me, and what would he tell my husband if I were lost? Lakshman took my arm as we crossed the tracks so we could board the train on the other side. I was still panting.

As we walked past car after car, I noticed the cars weren't air conditioned. People were hanging out of the opened windows. Oh, my, I thought, please let our car be air conditioned. After all this, I'm going to collapse if I don't have air. Thankfully, our car did have air conditioning.

The luggage was tossed overhead onto metal racks that didn't look like they would restrain the bags very well if we had to stop suddenly. I had visions of heavy bags being hurtled down upon us in our seats. Once I sat down, I observed the rather Spartan condition of the train. It had seats, ceiling fans, windows and a luggage rack, but it didn't come close to resembling our Amtrak back home. I had to take a picture of the interior to show my husband after all the wonderful trips we took on Amtrak from Florida to New York City.

A young man periodically walked up and down the aisle trying to sell food to us. Tomato soup, drinks, ice cream, and I think there was a full meal on a plate. I purchased the soup, thinking it would soothe my tummy. What the soup lacked in thickness it made up for in spices. Hot! Fortunately, I didn't get sick.

Later, Tim advised me to avoid the toilets. One of the toilet doors did not close properly and the other was a typical Indian toilet, something I had never seen before. An Indian toilet is best described as a hole that one squats over. I would pass on that experience, unless absolutely necessary.

It was probably five hours that we traveled on the train before we entered the station at Haridwar. I stepped off the train to be met by a commotion of people. I wasn't sure where to go until I saw a woman waving and yelling my name. She looked friendly and white, so I guessed her to be Helen from Australia. I was right. Helen grabbed me up in her arms, welcoming me to India. She put a garland around my neck as is the custom of welcome.

I noticed Tim behind me becoming emotional as he stood in the train station. He was finally in Haridwar, placing his feet on its soil, his dream of so many years finally being realized. A very moving experience for him, as I had anticipated it would be.

The four of us, Lakshman, Helen, Thapa and other assistants from the ashram walked us through the terminal to the parking lot. I was amazed at all the people lying on blankets on the floor of the train station. They were everywhere! I asked Helen about this and she told me that they were either waiting for their train to arrive or they would sleep there for the night. Once outside the terminal, it was more of the same. People were all over the ground, lying on blankets, sitting on blankets and eating on blankets, some alone and some with their children. Voices rose, speaking in Hindi, a language I was totally unfamiliar with. So, this is Haridwar, my new home for the next week. Oh, what an adventure this will be!

If this energy, this soul, this Word of God, enters a non-living thing, it becomes living, aware. If that energy leaves a living being, the creature dies.
Shri Satpal Ji Maharaj

Chapter Three
The Ashram Experience

After a short drive from the train station, we were finally at our intended destination, Prem Nagar Ashram. Our driver steered us through the entrance gates, past the guard's station, then down a long driveway. To the right of the driveway was a large manicured garden area. Just beyond the garden, we could see a portion of the enclosing walls that surround the compound. On the left side of the driveway was a series of attached buildings that act as offices, stores and a pharmacy. Beyond that was one of the residential buildings, about three stories tall.

The driver made a turn to the right, about midway in the compound, where we saw the main residential building that we would be staying in for the week, which is also three stories in height. This is where the holy family resides when they are in residence and some of the Mahatmas. Across from this building is a temple where the ashes of the founder, Satguru Shri Hans Ji Maharaj, and his wife, Jagat Janani Shri Mata Ji, are buried. It is a grand temple that followers visit often to show their respect. A mammoth auditorium is nearby where all the major programs take place at this ashram.

Many tarps were erected throughout the compound, intended to provide cover from the elements in anticipation of the thousands who would attend the two day birthday celebration for Satguru Shri Satpal Ji Maharaj, the son of the founder and creator of the ashram. After the celebration ends, the rented tarps and poles will be disassembled and the entire area will return to normal.

Our luggage was manually hoisted by assistants up two flights of stairs to the top floor where all four of us would be staying. I was enamored at the sight of this uniquely constructed interior as we followed behind our luggage, climbing approximately ten steep steps, crossing a landing, and then climbing about the same number of steps again, and that was just the first flight. There were no elevators. I was puffing by the time I arrived at the top floor, but that's okay. I can use the exercise.

Once at the very top, I realized that the large center area had no roof, so it's wide open to the sky. Directly in the center was a space that had a railing around it, allowing one to look over the railing to view all the way down to the first floor. I was told that when it rains, the rainwater washes away dirt and dust from the concrete surface, so there is a practical reason for the building being constructed in this manner. A cleansing actually takes place every time it rains.

There were wide-open sections on two sides of the building from which one could view the compound while looking out over the half wall. A trough ran along one wall where spigots were attached. This is where washing of dishes, pots and utensils is performed.

Two hallways on the left side ran parallel to each other, extending down from the open sections. Here there were rooms available for visitors. In between the two hallways was a large assembly area, and at the end of the hallways, running crossways, was a screened section where I suspected workers stayed during programs. There was a communal shower area available for those who stayed there.

To the right of the central area was a very large, open space that had been divided into smaller rooms by brightly colored sheets of cloth hanging from the ceiling. This division provided rooms for us to dine, along with areas for meals to be prepared. There were also several rooms available on the right side in which people could reside, similar to the ones located in the two hallways on the left side. Shri Vibhu Ji Maharaj would be staying in this area. Maharaj Ji and Mata Ji were on the second floor. Each had their own personal living space in which to receive people.

Three rooms were situated down our hallway. Helen and I shared the first and smallest room. The second room had four people who had come from Guadalajara, Mexico, and the last room was where my three traveling companions stayed. These two rooms were large and could accommodate numerous people, depending upon them not minding sharing a king size bed. Two of my three guys were fortunate to have a king bed all to themselves, while Dr. T had a single bed. There were also two couches and a chair to lounge in and a private bath in their room. The people from Mexico, three women and one man, had three king beds, a couch and some chairs, with a private bath.

The room Helen and I shared had three single beds that were pushed together, and a chair. We took the two outside beds to sleep in and left the center one for sitting or throwing our stuff on. We also had a private bath, and that's a story unto itself.

We were blessed to have what is called a Western toilet, which means, it looked like a regular toilet that we are all familiar with in the United States. The distinction is drawn between the Indian toilet, which I mentioned previously, the hole-in-the-floor variety. Nice Indian toilets have some tile along the sides where one would position the feet when straddling it. A normal looking sink was also in the bathroom.

The shower was unique, but functional. Everything was wide open because there was not an actual shower stall. The floor slanted slightly to cause the water to run toward the drain. A showerhead jutted out of the wall from way up high and cascaded the water directly downward. No adjustment could be made to the showerhead because it was situated too high. There was also a low faucet and a bucket in case one wanted to bathe Indian style. Some Indian people prefer to wash using a bucket rather than a shower. I remembered there being a bucket with a small cup provided at the hotel, also. I had wondered at the time why that was there.

We were fortunate to have a window air conditioning unit, like the other two rooms, and a ceiling fan. I came to highly appreciate the ability of a ceiling fan to keep us somewhat comfortable because elsewhere on our floor there wasn't any air conditioning. Our only means of attempted comfort from the heat was the overhead fans. Wherever we shared our meals, we had a ceiling fan. Some days that was adequate and other days, not so much. While we were in India, the temperatures were well into the 90s and the humidity was off the chart. It was *hot*! There were times when a pair of shorts and a halter top would have been desirable. But, we were in India and that meant our bodies had to be covered.

The food at the ashram was incredible, although a bit heavy on starch. The dishes we were served varied but, for the most part, contained lentils in different forms, lots of rice variations, potatoes, cauliflower, toast, cucumber and tomatoes, and chapatis. And, of course, lots of sweets, everything from cakes to puddings and a ball shaped concoction of sugary delight. Chutneys were available if you wanted to enhance the flavor of something or add some heat to it. Many of the dishes were very spicy anyway, but there were adequate numbers of dishes that were milder. We certainly did not want for anything to eat, quite the contrary! We were given such large portions three times a day that I became concerned about gaining weight. But due to the stair climbing, having to hoist myself into the SUV, and the walking we did, I actually lost a couple pounds.

With so many residents staying in the building during the birthday celebration, rather than one central location for food preparation, cooking was done on our floor for only those of us staying on the third floor. Enormous kettles, the size of which I've never seen before, were used to prepare our meals. A dozen or more dedicated women could be seen sitting on the cement floor in the center area working dough with their hands, while others were plopping the patties on a grill to cook them. It was a fascinating sight to see these women, of varying ages, all dressed in brightly colored saris, heads covered with scarves, manipulating dough between their palms that would later be eaten by us in the form of warm chapatis.

Each morning around 7:30 we would receive a knock on the door of our room to let us know that tea was being served. Sometimes we all gathered for tea, and other times the tea was left on a tray outside our door for us to bring into our room. We had breakfast mostly around 8:30. However, sometimes we had satsang at 9:00, so we had to hustle to eat or else satsang was delayed.

If we were in the building, we had lunch around 12:00, but if we were on a field trip, it could be at anytime we could find a place to eat or fit it into our schedule. Tea was always served around 4:00, depending what we were doing that day, along with cookies or something light to munch on. Dinner was at 6:00, unless Shri Vibhu Ji Maharaj or Mahatma Ji Fakiranand gave us satsang, or we had to attend something for the birthday celebration, and then it could be as late as 9:30 or 10:00 at night. Sometimes I skipped dinner at this late hour because lunch had been so late and the meal had been very filling, or I would just have dessert. Suffice to say, I never went hungry.

All the people who served us did so with love. Not

once did I see someone roll his or her eyes or hesitate for an instant to respond to a request. There was one lovely gentleman with gray hair and a pleasant smile on his face who would appear out of nowhere to assist me every time with the latch on my door. I am horizontally challenged, as they say, so I could not reach the latch to shove it closed or bring it down to unlatch. Suddenly, there he'd be, at my side to assist me. And he did it with kindness and love.

I found out from Helen that in his normal life he is a school bus driver, but came to Prem Nagar for the celebration and to serve his master. Like many, many others, this was an opportunity to serve Satguru Shri Satpal Ji Maharaj. The man was not paid to be of service, rather, he freely donated his time because he was serving his Satguru, expressing his love for him through service.

For an event of this magnitude that attracted approximately thirty thousand devotees, it was necessary to have people to do food preparation, cooking, cleanup, security and heaven knows what else. Everyone who devoted his or her time did so freely and with love. They were not paid to serve others.

I felt like I was surrounded by love. Everyone displayed loving gestures, smiled, laughed and was egoless. Being around people without ego was a circumstance unfamiliar to me. We human beings demonstrate daily what it means to have an ego. If we observe the behavior of our coworkers, friends and family, we will see ego displayed everyday in every way. But not these people, these devotees. There was no ego present that I observed. I was impressed.

Through my years of studies in spiritual matters, the ego has often been brought up for discussion. We are normally cautioned about exhibiting too much ego, and then some author comes along with a book that defends the ego, saying, ego gets a bad rap. Ego is what gives us determination to succeed. Ego gives us the self-confidence we need to survive in the material world, and so forth.

Personally, the egoless attitudes I witnessed were far more pleasant to be associating with than the bombastic egos back home. There was something positive in the idea of desiring to have less ego.

The first evening at Prem Nagar, we met Mahatma Ji Fakiranand, an elderly man with the smoothest skin I'd ever seen on a face belonging to one nearing eighty. He appeared very thin despite being dressed in a billowy, diaphanous orange robe, with a matching scarf draped over his baldhead. His smile revealed nice teeth, and I thought he was beautiful as he sat cross-legged on a chair in the room that the four people from Mexico occupied. Eight of us were seated on the floor, cross-legged, to hear our first satsang from this kind soul who would teach us about Knowledge. Three of us, Dr. T, Albert and I, had not been initiated, the rest had been in previous years. Experiencing satsangs was the way we would know if we wanted to be initiated.

After introductions, Mahatma Ji addressed Dr. T and then me, sort of giving us a heads up of what to expect during satsangs, preparing us for Knowledge. I paid close attention as he spoke because his accent was very heavy and he spoke softly. At the end of our visit, several came up to him, bent down to the floor and either touched his bare feet with their hands or with their forehead. I wasn't sure what that was about, but I would find out soon.

We left for dinner and returned afterwards for more satsang with Mahatma Ji. He addressed each of us newbies, non-initiates, individually, and the words he used indicated he knew exactly who we were and we were not going to fool him for one instant. He saw into our hearts and knew with certainty if we were present with sincerity or if this was just another lark in our spiritual/psychic adventures. I'm not sure if the other two grasped that fact immediately, but I received the message loud and clear. I accepted the fact that he had the ability to see the true me and prepared myself to be stripped naked of any pretenses or secrets.

Mahatma Ji mentioned to me that I talk to spirits, recognizing that I am a medium, but he said that there is so much more. Then he said to put my worldly ways behind me. I wasn't sure what area of my life he was speaking about because that could be interpreted into several areas, but then he mentioned the word social. I took that to mean I needed to stop the martinis every night when I get home from work. Message received.

Our teacher went onto explain about having a master, a guru. Guru is a Sanskrit word. Gu means darkness and ru means light. The guru leads one from darkness into light. He said that a master shows the way to God and through the living master one finds enlightenment and comes to know the self. That was exactly why I was here; I wanted to be shown the way.

Again, people lined up to touch the feet of Mahatma Ji. This custom is quite unfamiliar in the US. We would never do such a thing, probably thinking, "Why would I want to touch your feet? You are no better than me."

Touching the feet of Maharaj Ji or Mahatma Ji or any other holy person shows humility. We put aside our egoistical behaviors to recognize someone who is above us, someone who is holy. We are showing respect by touching their feet with our hands or forehead. We are humbling ourselves in the presence of holiness. I saw this as a good lesson in working through the unmerciful hold that the ego has on us.

Another reason the touching of the feet is practiced is for a transfer of energy. The head represents the North polarity, the feet the South polarity. A devotee places his or her forehead, the North pole, to the feet, South pole, of the holy one which causes a magnetic attraction to begin a flow of energy to the devotee from the holy one.

That evening helped me realize more clearly that the ego has a hold on all of us. It seemed, in reflection, that back home every time I turned around, the ego was rearing its ugly head. A thought occurred to me that the ego corrals us into limiting fences of activity, restricting us from breaking free of the mold, thinking outside the box, as they say. Therefore, the ego restrains us from liberation, from happiness. When we pay attention, we are able to recognize the mischievous patterns of the ego. That's the beginning of putting the impudent little brat in its place, by recognizing its presence.

The next morning after breakfast, the four of us were driven to the residence of Maharaj Ji in Dehra Dun,

Me, Dr. T, Shri Satpal Ji Maharaj, Albert and Tim

about two hours away from Haridwar. A high security wall surrounded the compound and there were guards dressed in uniforms at the gate who motioned us through. Three large buildings were inside: the guards' quarters, being the smallest structure; the office and the residence of the holy family.

Satguru Shri Satpal Ji Maharaj came out to greet us. He offered to pose for pictures to be taken using all of our cameras, which we eagerly accepted. Then we were escorted inside the office building, which appeared to be two stories, after leaving our sandals outside. It is the custom in India to be barefoot when indoors. We were always barefoot inside the ashram.

Tea and cake were offered after Maharaj Ji left us. Once we finished our snack, we were off to visit Mussoorie, which is close by Dehra Dun. We traveled up into the mountains, winding around on the narrow roads until we reached the peak, Mussoorie. Maharaj Ji had told the driver not to drive as fast as he normally would have around the mountain roads. It seemed pretty fast to me as the wonderful views of lush green trees and villages nestled into the mountains flew by as we sped along. Then the clouds rolled in and visibility below was poor.

This was obviously a tourist destination. Many hotels were inserted into the side of the mountain, perched high for optimal views of the Doon Valley. The streets were lined with a multitude of vendors offering wares such as wooden hand carvings, candleholders, bowls, jewelry, clothing and lots of shawls. Anything you could have conceivably wanted to buy in India was here.

We returned to Dehra Dun much later than was expected because we walked around, shopping in Mussoorie, way past the time our friend, Lakshman, had scheduled. He finally was able to corral all of us into the SUV.

Lakshman, who I've been mentioning, is the personal assistant to Maharaj Ji on all matters. He traveled with us for the majority of the time we were in India, which he considered to be a treat. Married, with one daughter, and perhaps in his early forties, Lakshman interpreted the language for us and advised us on so many issues. We came to look to Lakshman for everything as we considered him all knowing and simply a wonderful friend.

Upon our return, we kicked off our shoes and entered the personal office of Maharaj Ji again where we were served lunch. It was around 4:00 p.m. by this time. Just as we were ready to drive back to Haridwar, we were told to wait, so we walked around the garden area. Finally we were told that Maharaj Ji wanted to ride back to Haridwar with us, but he had to finish some business first.

So we waited some more, rather excited for this opportunity to spend time with the Satguru. His wife, Mata Shri Amrita Ji, we saw leave for Prem Nagar earlier in a separate vehicle. Eventually, there were seven of us, including the driver and Lakshman, riding back to Haridwar.

Driving close behind us was a vehicle filled with luggage, a few guards and a driver. Once when we were stuck in traffic in Dehra Dun, the guards started flashing lights and ran the siren to clear the cars and bikes so we would be allowed to move forward.

During the ride, Maharaj Ji gave Tim and me his personal cell phone so we could call home. Can you imagine that? I was finally able to talk to my husband and find out about two important issues. How was our ailing, old cat, and how is your mother? Both had been ill when I left, but were fine now, so no worries there.

Along the way back we stopped at a Buddhist temple to take pictures. The monks had just closed the temple for the evening, but we were welcomed to climb the long stairway to the landing—in our bare feet. It was a rough climb with the debris, sticks and whatever else one could imagine collected there, and because it was now dark, we couldn't see to avoid stepping on something. We took pictures of the building, which was lit by strands of lights, and the beautiful murals on the exterior wall on the landing, and then made our way back down the stairs.

During the drive, we again were regaled with stories about Tim and Albert's escapades during the previous night. They didn't appear to be sleeping much, perhaps too excited, because at 2 a.m. they again woke up and decided to walk down to the Ganges River. But this trip turned into a wet experience. Someone pushed Albert into the Ganges, which would have been a task with him being such a big fellow. Boys will be boys!

When we drove into the compound, the crowd that had gathered over night and during the day somehow knew this was Maharaj Ji's vehicle. They started praising him, loudly. I was impressed by this show of devotion, although it was a bit intimidating because of the size of the crowd. Maharaj Ji quickly disappeared, it seemed, into thin air, and we were whisked away from the mass of devotees.

When we got to the top floor, we discovered that our meal was being prepared. I was too full to eat a meal, so I just had the delicious pudding. Then I saw Mahatma Ji and he asked how I was, what we did and saw that day? Oh, he is the sweetest man! I just adore him! Then he told me to put aside my material world and blessed me twice by touching my forehead with his palm placed over my third eye. How terribly I will come to miss these blessings when I return home.

Helen has been making annual treks to this ashram for many years, even living there for ten years while she worked as a teacher in the ashram. She described the daily ashram schedule as being quite organized, with people waking up bright and early at 4 a.m. By 5 a.m., everyone has assembled on the first floor in the temple room for Arti. Arti is a very ancient ritual hymn. It can be heard in various forms in temples throughout India and is broadcast over loudspeakers during the famous "Arti to the Ganges" every evening in Haridwar. Although the melody is simple, it creates an uplifting affect. Devotees wave trays filled with candles and flowers before pictures or statues of their favorite deity. This hymn is also adapted for praising one's spiritual Master. The morning Arti at Prem Nagar is followed by thirty minutes of meditation.

Breakfast is at 6 a.m. or a bit later in the winter months. Everyone by 7:30 is beginning their service, ashram tasks, that is, for the day. Lunch is at midday, followed by rest until 2 p.m. Then everyone resumes their service, referred to as sewa, until 4:30 or 5 p.m., depending on the season.

Arti is again presented at 7 p.m., followed by satsang from 7:30 until 8:30. Dinner is served around 8:45

or 9:00, depending if the chapatis are ready. After dinner people get together to chat or go for a walk, eventually drifting back to their rooms to rest, read or whatever they wish.

The daily routine is punctuated by festival days, such as Krishna Janamashtmi, when a big feast is prepared, often sponsored by local or visiting Premies. Premie is the name given to people who have received Knowledge. Many non-premie visitors come to the ashram as pilgrims to spend a few days while making their rounds on the pilgrim circuit around Haridwar, Rishikesh and up onto Badrinath, Kedarnath, etc. They sometimes sponsor a lunchtime feast as they regard it as good karma to feed ashram residents and Mahatmas.

***

The next morning we discovered that Albert was not well. His feet and ankles were so swollen that when Maharaj Ji heard about his ailment, he said that Albert must go to the doctor, declaring that this had gone beyond the control of homeopathic medicine. But Albert was having no part of this suggestion, fiercely resisting a doctor's visit. After several of us talked to him, he relented.

All of us piled into the SUV and drove to a small hospital a few blocks away. With Lakshman guiding the process, the doctor saw Albert quickly while we waited in the vehicle. The diagnosis was edema. Both men came down the stairs and Albert stood in line at the open-air pharmacy to receive his medicine. The price was insanely cheap, like a couple dollars, as I remember. Later, poor Albert broke out in blisters all over his legs due to the heavy water retention.

After returning to the ashram, Lakshman took Dr. T and me on a shopping and sightseeing adventure within the ashram grounds. With so many people present within the compound, he did not want us roaming around alone due to a potential risk because we were foreigners. Dr. T is not a young man and I am a very small woman, as opposed to the large physiques of Albert and Tim. Both of these men, especially Tim, made it a habit to take off whenever they wanted, regardless of what Lakshman advised. But the chances of them being accosted were pretty slim. I was perfectly agreeable to following Lakshman's advice.

The tour of the compound gave me the opportunity to take some great photos of those who had gathered there for the celebration. It was as crowded as the streets of New York City. Everyone was intent on getting from one spot to another, totally ignoring anyone around him or her. We quickly learned that most of these Indians had not been taught Western courtesy. When I bumped into someone, I quickly excused myself. The person just looked at me curiously. But when an Indian bumped into me, no apologies were forthcoming. I was merely an object in their way, and off they would go, oblivious to the encounter. We just had different customs. It didn't bother me at all.

Dr. T and I purchased photographs of Shri Satpal Ji Maharaj and a few books written in English that were authored by Maharaj Ji. Clothes, shawls, blankets, scarves and various paraphernalia were also offered by vendors.

Lakshman showed us a huge tree where five trees

had entwined and grown together to produce this unique singular tree with different leaves on its branches. We passed a huge tarp-covered area where food preparation was done for the masses in attendance. I snapped pictures of men stirring an enormous pot who were willing participants to have their pictures taken. In another area, a large number of women were gathered preparing chapatis, all seated on the ground in their brightly colored saris. Some looked my way and smiled, others ignored me. What a colorful photo!

Along the path, people had flung their clothes and blankets over bushes or low fences to dry in the sun. More people were washing dishes in a trough, while others sat or lay on blankets out in the open. It was a remarkable sight to observe how these people coped with the intense heat and the conditions that any Westerner would have declared intolerable. I had my trusty hand fan and I was waving it for all it was worth to stimulate some breeze, no matter how slight.

The only convenience of sorts these people had was the two large buildings that housed four hundred toilets for just this type of event. I never entered the buildings to see if they offered Western or Indian toilets, and it never occurred to me to ask. My guess is they were Indian toilets.

Later that evening we had satsang with Shri Vibhu Ji in his quarters, which was a delight. This was the first time I had seen him since his visit to Cassadaga. Besides the four of us, Helen, and the four from Mexico, several new faces appeared from other countries. We were all foreigners to India, but held one thing in common, a love for Vibhu Ji.

It was a wonderful discourse in which he emphasized the importance of spiritual discipline. We are asked after initiation to meditate both morning and night. That takes discipline. He explained that discipline is learning, thereby putting a positive spin on something that could have rigorous connotations. Shri Vibhu Ji said that we didn't have to constrict ourselves by certain rules or ideologies. When we meditate and go deeper into ourselves, we learn from our true selves, which is the cosmic Knowledge that is already within us.

Shri Vibhu Ji went on to say that we commonly focus on spiritual traditions, spiritual obligations and practices, how we behave and so forth, all these things that are external to us, instead of the inner Self. The Self is not limited to the I or the mine, to individuals or names. The Self is the Pure Self that is unchanging, which is the image of God within all of us. By focusing on the external we miss out on what is the most important force: *what you already are.* By focusing through the intellect we will never realize our True Self.

One of the greatest philosophies of spirituality teaches us that we are complete in ourselves; it is just that we do not know it. All are given a spiritual force that is present inside that is beyond time and limitations, beyond anything that is restrictive. The Self is the pure identity because it is the source of our being; it is the source of everything in this world, which we call the True Self. Unfortunately, because of the influence of ignorance on the mind, it becomes difficult to see, but when Knowledge is given to us, which is inherent within all of us, through spiritual practice, through the techniques, we are able to activate that Knowledge. And when that Knowledge is charged and active, changes happen from within. The best part is, these changes are real changes because they have manifested from within the being, from within the core of our beings.

All of us were so enthralled with the discourse. We felt so privileged to have been in the presence of Shri Vibhu Ji and to have received such a wonderful satsang. My admiration for him is reinforced again. He is such a special person.

After our satsang, we prepared for the first night of the birthday celebrations.

When an aspirant is initiated into Knowledge, he has direct access to the Divine energy within himself.
Shri Satpal Ji Maharaj

Chapter Four
Happy Birthday

Helen and I dressed to attend the first birthday celebration event. She wore an authentic outfit, one of many she had purchased over the years. I wore Western clothing I had brought from home. All of us gathered together so we could be escorted to the auditorium. Another precaution since we were foreigners. Albert did not go with us because he still didn't feel well.

Once outside, I saw thousands of people attempting to get inside the auditorium, so there was a bit of pandemonium. I was a little intimidated by the density of the crowd and because it had gotten darker, so I followed closely since I wasn't sure where we were going. Dr. T extended his arm back towards me so I could take his hand.

When we entered the auditorium, we kicked off our sandals. The building was tightly packed with thousands seated on the floor to our left. The faces were like stones in a continuous wall of people. A stage was located at the center right of the building from where we entered. On either side of the stage was a platform. The Mahatmas were seated to the left and to the right were the Mahatma Bai Jis. Helen told me that Shri Satpal Ji created some waves when he started allowing women to be in the holy order, equal to the male Mahatmas. My feminist tendencies thought, good for him!

We were directed to be seated in the very front of a special grouping of chairs situated at an angle beside the Bai Jis. Because we were considered V.I.P.s, we were given special seating that enabled us to view everything without anyone blocking our view. The chairs were covered in velvet and were so wide, I could place my camera, notebook and fan beside me. Two of us could have shared each chair.

The masses in the audience who were seated on the floor were crammed in next to each other as close as they could sit, cross-legged, and equally close from their front to back. Uniformed, unarmed guards were dispersed in the front row to contain the crowd. Some hand fans twirled in the air in an attempt to circulate a breeze. While we may have had preferential seating, there was one equalizing factor: we were all going to perspire together. There was no air conditioning and it was probably well into the 90 degree range inside the building. A floor fan was pointed in our direction, but that was like trying to cool a desert with one air conditioner. Futile.

I was amazed at the display of orange flowers that were strung together and then looped against the back wall of the stage. Large clusters of orange, yellow and white flowers were attached to the same wall at varying positions. More beautiful arrangements of orange and yellow were in stands situated in between the seats of the holy family. It was a magnificent and brilliant sight to see so many lush flower arrangements at one time. Blending in with the color scheme, each of the holy family's chairs was draped with orange fabric. It was a sensory smorgasbord of colors, scents and excitement. I was numbed by the experience.

The holy family entered and a cheer went up from the crowd in praise of them. Satguru Shri Satpal Ji Maharaj was seated in the center with Shri Vibhu Ji Maharaj to the left and Shri Mata Ji Amriti seated to the right. She was dressed in an orange sari and scarf, while her husband and son were in white. A line of people entered from the left of the stage to place garlands of flowers around the neck of each member of the family. Each person who delivered a garland bent to touch the feet of whomever he or she had draped the garland around. This was a very loving gesture. I'm sure it was an honor to be chosen to do this.

Satguru Shri Satpal Ji Maharaj began to speak to the audience in Hindi. He had a pleasant public speaking voice. We placed headphones over our ears so we could understand what he was saying as Helen translated into our ears. A few years ago Helen learned the language so she could translate books into English for Premies. Helen did an admirable job of conveying what Shri Satpal was saying. After a bit of time, music was performed and a person sang through most of it in Hindi. Then the music became very lively and people in the audience began to dance. Much waving of arms took place and movement of hips. We were encouraged to stand and dance, so we did. A woman seated a couple rows behind was familiar with the dance and showed me how to move my hands overhead.

Then Tim got an idea. He formed a conga line and started leading us around in front of our seating. But that was not good enough for Tim. The next thing we knew, he was leading us to the very center of the area in front of the stage so that Maharaj Ji could see us, not to mention the thousands of devotees in the audience. The thought crossed my mind that these people are going to think we are a bunch of loony Americans. Fortunately, Maharaj Ji thought it was amusing, which it was, frankly, and a smile cracked his normally serious face.

Then Tim became bolder and led the conga line all the way across the front area of the stage to the Mahatmas, who he enticed to get up and dance. That didn't work. However, the Bai Jis took the hint and began dancing.

After a while, we were all panting and perspiring profusely, but we certainly did have fun dancing. I'm sure the group last year didn't demonstrate such abandon during the music!

We gathered again to make our departure, grabbing our sandals where we left them before exiting. Again, it was a smashing crowd of people, so Dr. T called out to me and clasped my hand in his so I didn't get trampled by the crowd. When we got upstairs to our quarters, our dinner was being served at 10:30 p.m. There was no problem eating at that hour because we had worked up an appetite from all the dancing. When we returned to our rooms, I had my second shower of the day, using pretty much all cold water. It felt grand!

While all of us slept, Tim went on one of his wee-hours-of-the-night treks. He struck up a conversation with a man who was a tribal Maharaj Ji who had come down from the mountains after a long meditative period to join in the birthday celebration. They sat on some steps across from the ashram and smoked and talked. Except the man did not speak English, and Tim did not speak whatever language it was that the man spoke. Somehow they managed to have a conversation for hours and that encounter spiritually affected Tim greatly. I continued to be amazed at the camaraderie that Tim was able to create with total strangers!

***

The second day of the birthday celebration began with Satguru Shri Satpal Ji Maharaj receiving his annual astrology reading. Helen led us to the auditorium where we sat on the opposite side from where we were located the previous night. We sat beside the area that had the video equipment. All events are taped and this was no exception.

The astrology reading had already begun, although we could not understand one word that was being said by the astrologer since he spoke either in Hindi or Sanskrit. Maharaj Ji was seated on the floor flanked on either side by his wife and son as the astrologer addressed him. The two men wore gold while Mata Ji wore orange. They sat under a four post apparatus with each post wrapped in gold fabric. Gauze material was stretched overhead, and orange and green flowers were strung together and looped all around the top border. Large bouquets of orange, yellow and white flowers punctuated each high corner of the apparatus.

Lakshman came up to us to invite us onto the stage to take pictures. Several of us walked around back of the Mahatmas where we climbed stairs to reach the side of the stage. From there we took close up pictures of the reading. I felt pretty special and appreciative to be allowed so close to the ceremony.

After returning to our seats, we accepted bottled water that was offered to us. Maharaj Ji then gave satsang to the audience in English, which was a real treat for us, and Shri Vibhu Ji followed by delivering satsang in Hindi. Mata Ji also gave satsang in Hindi. Being a woman myself, I truly enjoyed watching her delivery to the audience and hearing the tone of her voice. She did very well and it was obvious how much the people loved her. Tim videotaped the whole event.

Music and singing began, followed by Arti. The holy family each took a tray of candles and approached the altar on the back wall of the stage that had displayed on it pictures of Shri Han Ji Maharaj Ji and Shri Jagat Janani Mata Ji, the parents of Satguru Shri Satpal Ji Maharaj. They performed the ritual of waving the candles and flowers on the trays in front of the pictures to honor the parents and founders of the ashram. Chanting by others was also heard.

Bai Jis walked around with trays of candles so that the devotees could fan the smoke onto themselves as a blessing. Sweets were also distributed. When activity was beginning to wane, Helen attempted to herd us out of the building prior to the very end when it would be more chaotic. As I was walking in front of the stage towards the exit, a swarm of people came barreling through to receive blessings from the smoke of the Arti. I was caught in the middle of their intent, jostled all over the place, just an obstacle in their way. Finally, I was able to free myself and grab my sandals.

We lost the rest of the group, so Helen and I retraced our steps in an attempt to get to the back of the stage to avoid the crowd. The two of us battled our way toward the entrance of our building. Guards were pushing a couple people back from the entrance as they attempted entry where they did not belong. No badge, no entry. The stair climb to our floor seemed worse than usual, possibly due to the heat. By now I was thinking there were a minimum of twelve steps on either side of the landing. They're multiplying!

Once back in the room, I truly appreciated the air conditioning. It was brutally hot in the auditorium. I simply could not fathom how the devotees endured the heat when they were outside. But then it had been explained that these people were accustomed to the weather. Still, I felt bad for them.

While having lunch, I saw Mahatma Ji Fakiranand walking around. I approached him to ask if he would give me Knowledge. He smiled and said, yes. Then he asked when we were leaving and I told him Friday. He nodded, knowing he only had three days to fulfill my request. Okay, now I had committed myself. I was going to receive Knowledge. Helen and I rested for the remainder of the afternoon after having lunch.

Later that afternoon, Maharaj Ji invited all of us for a private visit. This gave us the opportunity to present him with his birthday gifts. My present was a copy of four of my books. He is an avid reader, as is Shri Vibhu Ji, although I questioned whether he would actually read any of my books, given the subject matter. He is so evolved from me that what I write about is mundane. But I never before had to figure out what to give a Spiritual Master for his birthday. I thought, perhaps this is an original gift.

When I presented Maharaj Ji with my gift, I told him I had purchased three of his books and I thought they were written to be easily understood. He seemed pleased by that. Tim later told me that he probably enjoyed hearing that comment because how many authors critique his work? Probably none.

Everyone chatted with Maharaj Ji briefly after presenting their gifts. I think I only said what I mentioned previously about the books. I never knew what to say to him. He usually wore a serious expression and is so highly evolved, I felt like a mere flea in his company.

While walking to the auditorium, Tim informed me that when I was seated directly in front of Maharaj Ji, the soles of my feet were pointing towards him, which is an insult. That comment knifed right through me. I was upset to the core of my being at the thought I had unintentionally insulted Maharaj Ji. What was worse, I knew better. I had read during my research somewhere that one does not direct the bottoms of the feet towards holy people because it is perceived as an insult. I had insulted Maharaj Ji! Great heavenly days, I was mortified! How could I have been so stupid? I didn't have to stretch my legs out in his direction, for crying out loud. What was I thinking?

After we were seated in the same location as the previous evening, I leaned across Dr. T toward Tim. I told him he should have signaled me at the time my errant feet were pointing in the wrong direction. Then my eyes welled up with emotion. Tim said that Maharaj Ji wouldn't have been insulted because he realizes that Westerners do not know the customs. But my emotions were running wild by then, given the surroundings, my heightened sensitivity and over the thought that I could even for a mere second have insulted Maharaj Ji.

Vibhu Ji was seated alone on the stage giving satsang. He spoke in Hindi, so we could not understand what he was saying. Afterwards, his parents entered and were seated amid praising from the audience. Then came the news that Lakshman had arranged for us to present garlands to the holy family, like the others had done the evening before. I was a little hesitant and still felt emotional, but I agreed to do it. It's an honor, how could I not do this?

A gentleman on the stage introduced us by name as foreign visitors, and then Lakshman led us outside and around to the back of the stage. We each were given a garland and told to walk out onto the stage and put the garland around one member of the holy family. We were at the opposite side of the stage from last night so we couldn't follow what they did previously. I was really intimidated. Heaven forbid I commit another faux pas.

I certainly did not want to present a garland to Maharaj Ji under the circumstances. So I walked out there, number three to go, feeling like, this is not where I want to be. I chose Mata Ji since she was closest and I felt a bit more comfortable going to her rather than having to cross in front of Maharaj Ji to get to Vibhu Ji. She smiled at me, such a pretty smile, and I dropped to my knees so I could touch her feet with my hands. At least that's what I think I did, although it could have been my forehead. After she smiled I sort of forgot everything. I wanted to leave the stage. Talk about feeling intimidated!

I felt such a rush of relief to be back outside. A couple of us then walked around and back inside to our seats. Once seated, I looked at Maharaj Ji and sent him a very sincere apology. I kept mentally sending out, I am so sorry to have unintentionally insulted you.

Our translator this time for Maharaj Ji's satsang was Lakshman. He did a beautiful job conveying the inspirational words that Maharaj Ji delivered to us. After he spoke, music was again performed and the audience stood to dance. Our little group danced somewhat, but I sat it out. Arti was the final activity. The lights were turned down and several Mahatmas were seated on the stage facing the holy family with their trays and candles. About six Bai Jis were seated on the floor in the center, directly in front of the audience, facing the holy family. It was all so lovely with the candles flickering, lighting the darkness. Symbolic as well, I think. Our Satguru leading us from the darkness into the light.

When everything ended, we picked up our sandals and made our way back to our rooms. What an experience!

Upon rising in the morning, I looked out the window. It was like a Tsunami swept through the ashram compound, taking with it all the tarps, poles and other paraphernalia that were necessary to provide comfort for the attendees. I discovered that even on our floor, the brightly colored and patterned cloth that had been hung to divide large areas into several smaller rooms had disappeared in the blink of an eye. It was like discovering a whole new floor! Everything was wide open now.

And then it rained. Helen said that every year, the day following the close of the birthday celebrations, it always rains. Sure enough, it was raining, cleansing the ashram so it could return to normal.

Everything seemed to have wound down to a gentle hum. So many people had apparently left during the night and now the rest were leaving from the grounds during the day. There was an entire shift in energy within the ashram to that of something more restful, more normal.

When I saw Albert and Dr. T I asked them if they wanted to receive Knowledge? Yes, both said that was their desire. So I informed them that they needed to ask to receive Knowledge because they did not know that was necessary. Both asked to receive Knowledge from Mahatma Ji Fakiranand. Now there were three of us. We have all had sufficient satsang, so we would begin the training.

We met each day in the morning and evening to learn the techniques for meditation and to practice the meditation. The first session began at 10 a.m. with satsang, followed by instruction, and ended at 3 p.m. The three of us made our dedication and received His grace from Satguru Shri Satpal Ji Maharaj through Mahatma Ji Fakiranand while the four Premies from Mexico, Tim and Helen witnessed our initiation. This is a life changing experience, very personal and secret.

When Mahatma Ji touched the top of my head, I felt the grace from Maharaj Ji flow throughout my entire body. We were being baptized into our new spiritual life and thus beginning a spiritual transformation. It was what I had wanted and anticipated, so I was thrilled to my core being.

Mahatma Ji asked me if I saw the light and I answered, yes. At first I saw a little pin prick of light, then it grew to lots of lights. Symbols followed, and then I saw a large silver light coming in from the left which grew into a giant jewel with many facets. The facets turned into colors. This was like nothing I had ever seen in previous meditations. Normally a teacher will instruct students to visualize a bright, white light, the brightest light they have ever seen. But there was no visualization involved. I *saw* with my third eye, as clear as clear can be. Nothing could compare in my past meditations to this experience. It was *real*.

Later, Mahatma Ji asked me if I heard anything, and I answered, yes. At first it sounded like flies buzzing, then frogs croaking. I could hear talking in a language I didn't understand coming from my left, which I presumed to be Hindi. Then I saw Maharaj Ji was the one talking. Temple bells chimed.

Thereafter in our sessions, nothing so dramatic occurred when I was supposed to hear. All I heard was a stringed instrument being played badly. As for seeing, further meditations revealed a brilliant light in the center that opened up suggesting to me that there was something beyond to see. It seems that we are usually more proficient in one or the other and I guess I am meant to see rather than hear.

These were my personal, individual experiences and are not meant to suggest that this is something someone else should use as a measure. I have always been taught that we should never compare ourselves to another. Each of us responds individually and receives in a manner we can best understand. Every person who receives Knowledge will do so in a manner that is perfect for him or her.

Afterwards, I was feeling so peaceful and blitzed out from the initiation and meditations. I was blessed to be in the presence of such a holy man as Mahatma Ji Fakiranand and to be receiving Knowledge through him in particular. He has been a Mahatma for forty years and has given Knowledge to over one hundred thousand people. I am in love with him, spiritually speaking.

I looked forward to having the opportunity to touch his feet every time I was in the room with him, which we did in the beginning and at the end of each session. It was an honor. We also touched our foreheads to the floor in front of a large picture of Maharaj Ji at the beginning and end of each session to show respect and love for our Satguru. Mahatma Ji Fakiranand did a full body prostration in front of the picture every time. He is supremely devoted to Maharaj Ji. That in itself was awe inspiring. He truly is a saint.

We were instructed to meditate twice a day for an hour and told that the more we meditate, the more we will gain. It is very important in the beginning to keep a regular meditation schedule to enhance our development. Synchronicity of occurrences was to be expected. Being a vegetarian was also stressed because it makes one lighter when meditating. Mahatma Ji Fakiranand asked the question, "Why would you want a graveyard in your stomach?" I loved that! I made a mental note that when I got home to share that question with my vegetarian employee. Now we would have a phrase to counter those who think it's weird to be a vegetarian.

Dr. T and I later decided to venture out into the streets of Haridwar. It was very crowded and there were lots of street vendors selling their wares. We ran into Tim while we were at the bank cashing Dr. T's traveler's checks. So, the three of us walked around and into some of the shoe stores. My feet are so small, I couldn't wear any of the shoes. Pity, I love shoes, like most women.

Then the three of us went into some jewelry stores. They did not sell 14 karat anything, only 22 karat gold, and maybe a little 18 karat. I wanted to purchase some hoop earrings, but hoops did not seem to be popular with Indian women because I didn't see any available. I was also looking for a gold toe ring, but no luck there either. One thing I thought was interesting was that they served us Chai tea in the jewelry stores. And it was delicious!

Over lunch, once again we were told about the adventures of Tim and Albert during the wee hours of the morning. As was usual for Tim, he had woken up in the middle of the night a couple nights previous, so, being awake, he decided to take a walk down to the Ganges River. He saw an area teaming with activity. Small groups were camped out along the streets leading to the river.

These people would be best described as marginal types who had chosen to camp there. It appeared to Tim that the women had gone to rest with the children while the men continued their activities.

Music pierced the night air like a siren warning of danger. Makeshift instruments were used, anything that would sound like a drum was thumped, or perhaps a pipe was struck to produce a musical note. A one-stringed instrument was played by a man. Everyone was joyous, singing, dancing and making merry. Tim was invited to participate by a man resembling those we have seen on TV who look like Taliban people. Having been a drummer at one time, Tim joined right in. He clapped and danced with everyone, adding his merry to theirs.

After awhile, things quieted down and the original man who had invited Tim into the group asked him if he'd like to have some tea? Sure, why not? Then the offer extended to walking outside the gated area to receive tea. This didn't feel correct to Tim. Something just wasn't right there. So he told the man that, no, he didn't want to leave the compound. Tim returned to the room shortly thereafter.

The next morning Tim had told Dr. T and Albert about his escapade during the wee hours. Albert asked, who were these people? Tim said he didn't know, for all he could guess they were the Taliban or whatever. But Albert didn't believe Tim, so he went out the next night with Tim to see for himself.

On this particular night, the entire scene had changed. The previous night's group had disbanded and in its place was another collection of makeshift accommodations. All combinations of people, all God's children, were camped out along the roads, conveniently near the Ganges. Similar to the night before, music hung heavy in the air like the humidity.

Albert and Tim were offered chairs to sit on. They obviously were very hot, so a couple young men came to them waving fans up and down at a rapid pace to cool them off. Even though they protested, everyone insisted they must be cool, so the fanning continued.

Albert and Tim enjoyed the music, so when a song ended, Tim shouted out, "Woo!" to show his appreciation. It was all he could figure to do so he could contribute to the festivities. Thereafter, whenever the music would stop, everyone else shouted, "Woo!" Woo became the call of the night and into the following day. Wherever Tim went in Haridwar, someone would hoot out, "Woo!"

Although it was announced that we were going on a field trip to the herb farm that the ashram owns on the outskirts of Haridwar, Helen, Dr. T, the four from Mexico and me were all who showed up. No one knew the whereabouts of Tim and Albert. They had a tendency to disappear anyway, so we went without them.

The farm was sixty acres and it produces all the herbs that are used in the Auyervedic medicines they have available at the ashram's pharmacy. A greenhouse in the center protects the rare herbs. Sugar cane, corn and other vegetables are also grown that sustain the ashram. Two buildings, a slight distance from the vegetation, house cows, bulls and calves. We took lots of pictures of the farm because it was so lovely. Some of the premies who work the farm live at the ashram.

While touring the farm, the humidity was so high, we soaked our clothes. All of us gathered after the tour to have tea while sitting under a gazebo-type building that had a fan. Ah, it was so hot, at last a breeze!

Again we met in the evening to have satsang, followed by more instruction. Mahatma Ji told us that the next morning we would meet for our last meditation. Mahatma Ji and the rest of us would be leaving afterwards. We would no longer be meeting with Mahatma Ji Fakiranand, which upset me terribly. I was a basket case by the close of the session. I touched my forehead to his feet and cried openly. I blubbered to him that I would miss him so much. He smiled and said, he would miss me and all of us more than I miss him. He is absolutely the dearest man, the epitome of love and a true saint. All I could do was sit there and cry because I knew after we left in the morning that it was a total mystery when I would have the opportunity to see this wonderful soul again. I cried all the way back to my room, too. I was an emotional mess.

During the final morning meditation, Mahatma Ji gave us our last instructions on being dedicated. Afterwards, we all went to pack. I was pretty much done packing, so I ventured out for a walk down to the Ganges. I saw Albert sitting on the side of the river, so I joined him. I had given him two vials with the request that he fill them with water from the Ganges. He held up the vials when he saw me, filled with Ganges water.

It is thought that the water from the Ganges is holy, so I felt I must take some home with me. The vials of water would hold a special place on my altar. However, I had no desire to get into the Ganges River in order to retrieve some water. One never knew what might come floating by. One might see trash, at the very least, or a carcass of an animal, most notably, a cow. Who knows what might travel that way? I did not want to tempt fate regarding contracting a disease from the Ganges River either, but since Albert had swum there numerous times, I knew he wouldn't mind collecting some water. He even swam a little in the ghat while I sat on the bench at that time.

While we sat at the side of the ghat watching two young boys swimming in the river, others joined later on, stripping outer clothing to get down to their "swim trunks," or whatever it was they wore. Most looked like they were dressed in underwear.

It was so pleasant sitting and watching nature and people, so peaceful and calm. The atmosphere was very distant from back home where there was always some hustle and bustle. And I don't even live in a large town. Other places would be far worse than where I reside. I don't think I could handle that much stress and commotion anymore from a large city.

When we were departing, everyone in the ashram gathered around. We took pictures with everyone and became emotional over our departure from our home away from home. When would we ever return? Ah, we said, next year, or maybe even sooner in February. Hm. I wonder.

All of us and our dear Helen.

We pulled forward in the SUV and saw Mahatma Ji just up ahead, so we stopped to say a final, final goodbye. He wanted to take pictures with all of us, so we all posed with him. Just one more time, I had to touch his feet. We all were crying by the time we left, except Tim. Apparently he had been out all night long walking around Haridwar, saying goodbye, so he wouldn't lose his composure today.

The train was on time and was first class. While the one coming to Haridwar had been marginal, this train was top of the line. We received what I thought was an odd dinner, but then a bit later it was followed by spicy tomato soup. The next thing we knew, we were served a full dinner. Apparently the first go round had been the appetizer. Ice cream followed a little while after the dinner was served. All this was included in the price of the train ticket.

About 11 p.m., we arrived in Delhi. Two guys carried our luggage from the train, balanced so gracefully on top of their heads. Imagine, our heavy luggage piled onto the top of the head! We waited at the curb for our driver to pick us up. And we waited amid all the commotion of the cars milling around. And we waited. Tim grew very irritated, finally declaring he was tired and wasn't waiting any longer. We weren't sure if it was his blood sugar going haywire that made him so impatient or the fact that Tim had stayed out all night saying goodbye to Haridwar. Whatever the reason, Tim took action. He hailed a taxi and then another because given the small size of the taxis, we needed two to carry all the luggage and us. The taxis cost $3 each in American money.

We gave instructions to go to the Guatam Hotel where we had stayed last week, assuming Lakshman had made reservations for us at that particular hotel. The traffic was very heavy, but it still seemed like it was taking an unusual amount of time to get to the hotel. Our driver started driving around similar streets, giving us the impression he was lost. Meanwhile, the other taxi was following us up and down the wrong streets. Finally, our driver pulled over to a curb, jumped out of the taxi and left Dr. T and me in the backseat as he sprinted across the street to a building. I said to Dr. T, "You do realize this could be viewed as suspicious?"

"Yes, it is," he replied.

"The driver takes off leaving us here, unprotected," I said, stating the obvious. "Thieves could be coming out of nowhere to rob us. He didn't even shut his door. This is right out of a movie."

"Oh, boy."

Fortunately for us, it was just my over active imagination creating this scenario. The driver came bounding back, jumped into the taxi and took us within a few minutes to the correct hotel. Whew!

We were relieved to find that we did have

reservations. The driver who was supposed to have picked us up at the station called at the front desk while we were checking in, asking to speak to Tim. But Tim refused to speak to him, so Dr. T took the call. The driver apologized profusely for forgetting to pick us up at the train station. He suggested that he come by the hotel in the morning at 7 a.m. for our trip to Agra. Tim decreed that time to be too early and we all agreed. We settled on 9 a.m.

Once again, I had my same room across from Albert and Tim. It was so nice to crash on the bed by myself, at last.

In the morning, Dr. T called Albert and Tim's room. A servant with a heavy accent spoke with him, much to Dr. T's surprise. When Dr. T went to their room, Albert greeted him with the accent he had used on the phone that made Dr. T think Albert was a servant. Dr. T cracked up.

At 10 a.m., Lakshman arrived with a different driver. We found out that the driver from last night who had been late arriving at the train station had panicked when we weren't there. Lakshman had yelled at him for his negligence. Ooh, poor man.

We stored our biggest bags at the hotel, choosing to travel with only a small one for quicker movement as we visited one place and another. Off we went on a whirlwind tour of some of the popular tourist sites. First stop, Agra, home of the Taj Mahal.

When the Word expands and resonates it is called Divine Music. When it further expands, it is transformed in Divine Light.
Shri Satpal Ji Maharaj

Chapter Five
On the Road Again

The four of us road in one SUV while Lakshman accompanied the four people from Mexico in another vehicle. Probably two hours had passed after leaving the hotel and, we were still in Delhi, on the Southside. It was much cleaner there and there were lots of beautiful looking apartments. Our driver, Ranjeet, told us that Delhi is older than Egypt.

We made one stop for gas and a restroom break. Here I was presented with the opportunity to use an Indian toilet. It wasn't horrible, just a bit awkward, and I had some tissue in my purse. Otherwise, it would have been a damp experience for sure.

Tim asked for a diet Coke, but none was available, as usual. Either it was the full strength version of Coke or diet Pepsi that was available, not that I wasn't fond of Diet Pepsi. It was Tim who was intent on the diet version of Coke in particular. At this point, I was thinking, India as a whole needs to stock up on Diet Coke.

After a few more hours, we stopped at a roadside restaurant and souvenir shop. They had a huge variety of paraphernalia to choose from, even elephant statues, as if anyone could squeeze that into a suitcase! Lakshman secured a table for us and presented a variety of chapati sandwiches he had brought. We ordered drinks from the establishment.

Albert was on a roll with his impersonations of an Indian. He kept mimicking the Hindi language, which was not impressing Lakshman one bit. Tim finally said something to Albert, along the lines that he was offending Lakshman. Albert buried his impersonations.

While we were driving on the last half of the trip to Agra, Ranjeet tried to teach Tim to count from one to ten in Hindi. Finally, we arrived at the Clark Shiraz Hotel. Security was tight. We were stopped at the gate so people could check the inside of the trunk and run a mirror attached to a pole under the front of the vehicle. Apparently they were looking for anything suspicious that was not normally located underneath a vehicle. Perhaps a bomb?

Once at the entrance, a very formally dressed man opened the door for us. He wore a purple uniform with a very tall hat complete with plume. We walked through a metal detector to enter the hotel, much like those found at the airport. This was a grand hotel! The lobby was huge, with chandeliers, beautiful carpeting and luxurious sofas. The rooms were absolutely gorgeous, too. Two king beds with lovely duvets on top, television, a beautiful, full facility bathroom and even a safe to store valuables. The cost for this room would have been $170 a night, but because we had connections, it was only $90 for pure luxury. Ah, yes, I like this!

After checking in, Lakshman hurried us out of the hotel so we could see the Agra Fort before it closed. Tomorrow we would see the Taj Mahal, so time was limited. The Agra Fort was built by Emperor Akbar in 1565 AD and it was quite impressive. Also impressing us was the barrage of little sales boys who immediately besieged us at first sight. Lakshman helped to dissuade the persistent boys as he escorted us towards the entrance. Tim, however, was more interested in networking with the boys. He lagged behind to talk with them, eventually meeting up with us about half way through the tour.

As we were leaving, we were again swarmed by the zealous sales boys. One pushed a carved object at me to buy and I refused. Another was right on his heels figuring I'd say yes to him, even though it was the same article! I turned around and jewelry was presented under my nose. It was becoming bedlam with so many boys hurling articles at us for purchase. Walking away didn't even help. No one would accept no for an answer.

Our driver finally came to our rescue and we climbed into the SUV. But the boys were still attempting to sell their wares, making it difficult to even close the doors. I was so relieved to be inside! Now I know what it must be like to have the paparazzi chasing you! The driver carefully pulled away to avoid running over someone.

We returned to the hotel, went through security inspections again, freshened up and left to go to dinner at a restaurant. The restaurant was very unique in that it was constructed with strips of wood displayed in designs on the ceiling. We enjoyed a wonderful Indian meal, although some Chinese dishes were also available. This was really nice after such a long drive from Delhi, followed by all the walking around at the fort. Relaxing back at the hotel was such a treat, too, especially since it was so luxurious and not the kind of accommodations any of us were used to.

I rose at 6:15 the next morning and we all left for the Taj Mahal at seven-ish. Lakshman warned that it would be terribly crowded, so we needed to get there very early to avoid some of the crowd and the intense heat. Lakshman was correct. By the time we left the Taj Mahal, it was really becoming too busy to enjoy the scenery or take pictures without someone's body appearing in the photo that wasn't supposed to be there.

We posed for professional pictures in a group and individually. One had me standing on a bench supposedly holding the Taj Mahal by a peak between my fingers. Silly stuff, but cute none the less.

The Taj Mahal was built in 1631 by Mughal Emperor Shahjahan in memory of his beloved queen, Mumtaz Mahal. Despite security risks in the past, we were allowed entry into the lower part of the Taj Mahal at this time, certain to be subject to change at any moment. It was a truly beautiful structure, created with love for another. It is a must to see when visiting India. Before I came, everyone was asking me if I would see the Taj Mahal. Well, I did! With its gleaming white exterior enhanced by the deep blue backdrop of the sky, it appeared like something straight out of a movie set, unreal in its elegant beauty.

Tim and Albert did not go into the building itself. Tim felt a strong pastlife connection and did not feel comfortable entering. Albert felt similarly and meditated on a bench with Tim while we made the tour and took pictures.

A bus returned us to the parking lot where beggars were pitifully asking for money. One child must have had scoliosis because his hip was so turned that one leg was bent and stuck out to the side. He walked on his hands and one knee. Sandals were attached to his hands and knee. Another boy was a duplicate, except I could tell he was faking his affliction. His body wasn't deformed and I knew I could get into the same position as he with no trouble. Others were blind or on crutches. I surmised that this was *the* place to beg because only "rich" people would come to the Taj Mahal from other countries. This is a sad and horrible way to live.

I remembered some of the scenes from the movie *Slumdog Millionaire*, which I made certain to see before coming to India, that were similar to this sight. In the movie children were maimed so they would appear more pitiful when begging. I wondered if any of these young souls had been tortured into becoming good candidates for a career in begging? The answer to that question I will never know.

We returned to the hotel for breakfast at 11 a.m. By 12:15 we were on the road again, heading to Jaipur where the shopping was supposed to be excellent. Along the way we stopped to gawk at a made-over truck that a poor Indian had transformed from nothing into something. Tim stood for picture taking with several boys who were more than eager to participate. They all smiled and appeared quite happy. Then some others approached the car to sell necklaces. They were quite pretty, so I purchased six to sell at the salon.

What was amazing was that no matter how poor some of these people were, they appeared happy. In their little worlds, happiness reigned, due to their sincere spiritual beliefs. The material world wasn't important to them, only the spiritual world held meaning. This was a lesson for Americans to observe during our time of economic crisis. All of us could do with less and should not complain. Those with jobs should be grateful and learn to live within their means instead of getting deeper into debt. India has much to teach us.

We continued to travel on a highway at whatever speed felt comfortable to the driver, as was everyone else. There were no speed limit signs posted. As a matter of fact, I realized I hadn't seen even one speed limit sign anywhere in India. There were toll booths, periodically, stopping us in our pursuit to reach Jaipur at a reasonable time, but nothing else slowed our journey.

Mud huts could be seen out our vehicle's windows. They had grass roofs in these small villages. We passed through cities, too, each being known for its particular architecture. Some cities were known for their sweets, and we were told that Jaipur is known as the pink city because its buildings are pinkish in color. However, once we arrived in Jaipur, the buildings actually appeared more peach than pink to me. It was a lovely city and one I would especially welcome the opportunity to visit again.

We stopped in an area Lakshman said was predominantly known to sell clothing. We all had a lot of fun there visiting the many shops. I purchased twenty-four bracelets to sell back home, three pairs of harem pants and two tops just for me. Everything was gloriously, brightly colored and so unique to anything I could buy in the States. Tim bought clothing for his wife and something for himself. Dr. T felt overwhelmed by the heavy handed salesmanship and some of us thought he might collapse, so he was taken by Lakshman to have tea across the street.

We joined them later for tea at a restaurant that was about three hundred years old. But it was a nightmare for me to cross the street and I was petrified, so Tim grabbed my hand to help me cross. After tea, we did it all over again.

At last we arrived at our hotel outside of the city, Chokhi Dhani Resorts, a five star ethnic village. This was a stunning hotel! It was like we were in the Arabian Nights. The lobby area was in one building, which was gorgeous beyond explanation. We were even served buttermilk as we checked in. I'm not a milk drinker and buttermilk wouldn't be my choice if I were. Politely, I sipped it to see if the taste had improved since the last time I tried a sampling when I was a child. Um, not so much.

We were led outside and down the pathways past other cottages and buildings to our two story building where the four of us were to share a suite. I had been asked if I was willing to share space with the three guys so we could cut expenses, but, sorry, I was not willing to be that intimate with three men who weren't my husband. Besides, we were receiving huge discounts at luxurious hotels and I do so love to stay in hotels.

Albert and Tim always stayed in one room during our travels and Dr. T and I each had a separate room. But this time we had a suite with two bedrooms. Double doors opened into a small living room with either bedroom to the side. The guys had one king bed, but they were bringing in a single bed. Tim was claiming the couch to sleep on and I had the other bedroom all to myself. We each had a large bathroom. My room was so gorgeous, I took pictures. And it only cost me $80 in American currency.

After we unpacked, we were leaving to tour the festivities and eat dinner when Maharaj Ji called on one of the working cell phones, which wasn't mine. It never worked in India. Tim talked first, and then Maharaj Ji asked to speak to me. I was thunderstruck to think he even knew my name. He asked me how I liked the tour? I said, it was wonderful, the hotels were great and this one was by far the best. I also thanked him for making all this possible. While I was trying to regain my composure, the others spoke with him.

We resumed our tour of the nightly festivities along with the throngs of families milling around. There were snake charmers, dancing girls, a tightrope walker and a palm reader for entertainment. It was all very delightful, but I was so tired and starving. Dr. T and I decided to skip dinner at a restaurant with the guys and go back to the room. I had some crackers stashed away that would sustain me well enough, besides, it was about 11 p.m. And I was more tired than hungry.

I shut my ornately, carved, wooden double doors to the living room area so I could have privacy. It was time for a shower. Unfortunately, the shower head, which was way up high, was pointed so the water leaked out of the tub. I placed towels around the base of the tub to collect the stray water and climbed in.

While washing my hair, all the lights went out. I was in pitch black darkness. I called out, "Master, let there be light!" A few seconds went by and the lights came back on. But in the meantime, I had knocked over the shower gel onto the floor, which was mixing with the water now flooding the bathroom. I hastened to finish so I could attend to the mess. Climbing out of the tub, I shut off the faucet and attempted to mop up the water and not fall on the slippery floor while doing it.

Next came the fiasco with the blower dryer. I was so delighted to see a blow dryer since my blow dryer had died in Delhi the first night. But I couldn't get it to work. No matter what I did, that dryer would not turn on. In the meantime, the shower decided to turn itself back on. Again I turned off the shower and returned to the dryer. Still no luck there and then the shower came on again. I couldn't shut the thing off this time and I just started laughing. I had a possessed bathroom!

I called room service, it must have been around midnight by then, laughing as I tried to tell them my shower wouldn't stay turned off. Could someone please come check it out? After I hung up it occurred to me that they probably thought I was nuts. Worse still, there I was, a woman, calling late at night about a shower—and I was laughing. They could think I was planning to seduce whoever came to my room.

I dressed sufficiently to receive the young man who was coming to my aid. But before he arrived, I tried again to turn off the shower and succeeded. Oh, no, now he really would think I was a nut case or out to seduce him!

The young man knocked on my door and I let him in. I told him that I had been able to shut off the shower, but maybe he should look at it anyway. He did and of course the shower was just fine now. So, I asked him to look at the blow dryer since he was there. The man touched the blow dryer and it sprung into action immediately. Oh, now I see, it has a pressure point that starts it. Somehow I must have missed it.

I really felt stupid, so I tipped him generously for his trouble. He left and I attempted to dry my hair again. The blow dryer didn't work! No matter what I did, that blow dryer was simply not going to respond for me. Laughing all the way out of the bathroom, I was convinced the room was possessed.

I wrote in my journal, meditated and watched a little TV before going to sleep. At that point I hadn't heard Albert and Tim come back to the room and never did.

In the morning we enjoyed a delicious breakfast buffet. Lakshman joined us about midway through our meal. He had stayed at the local ashram that night. After we checked out and took pictures in the lobby area, we drove to the Jaipur Ashram where we all fell in love with the residents.

Som Bai Ji is the elder Mahatma at the ashram, and Angali Bai Ji is the young one. There was another very young woman who was not dressed in the typical orange sari robes who had recently come to stay. She had a desire to be a Bai Ji. Another devotee lived there also.

This ashram is quite attractive and good sized. The main hall is large enough to hold probably several hundred people. The second story is where two guestrooms are located along with the quarters for the holy family when they are in residence. It was so peaceful there, I would love to return and stay for awhile.

Lakshman intended for us to move on after having lunch so we could see another fort, but Tim was so taken with Som Bai Ji and the ashram, he begged to remain longer. We all agreed, this is where we wanted to remain for awhile. Lakshman relented.

Som Bai Ji, who is approximately seventy-five to eighty years old, is such a tiny woman and child-like at times. She spoke with a heavy accent in a very girlish voice. Remarkably, there were no lines on her face. I was so drawn to this tiny woman and she appeared to be taken with me as well. At one point she stroked my face and hair with her hand. Som Bai Ji is such a sweetheart.

Tim had an idea to give her a teddy bear that his mother has given him as a goodbye gift. The bear had a red heart on its chest and when she squeezed it, the bear said, I love you. She was so cute, squeezing the bear and repeating afterwards, I love you, in her girlish voice. She kept hugging the bear and even shed a couple tears. What a dear, sweet soul she is.

We each received blessings from the two Bai Jis. Angali Bai Ji rubbed a red dot, called a tika or tilika, at our third eye and placed a garland around our necks. Som Bai Ji wrapped orange yarn around our wrists many times. This blessing is worn on the right wrist for men and the left for women. I was so touched to have received the blessings and to have met these lovely Bai Jis.

Lakshman hustled us along so we could make it to the last fort before it closed. This one was in Rajasthan. We arrived too late to ride a camel, but that was okay with me. It may have been fun, but it didn't break my heart not to have done it.

We hired a tour guide to show us through the amazing Amber Fort. It was huge! There were several floors and it went off in many directions. At one point, I looked at something for longer than I should and the others moved on. I had to guess which of two directions they went. I guessed wrong. I remembered the Delhi train station with amusement. *Should have turned right*! And once again, I should have turned right! But I was not the least bit concerned. I figured I could go up higher and look down to see where the group was located. Wrong again. It didn't matter that I was on the third level, I still could not see anyone familiar. But all along the way, I was enjoying seeing the fort.

Eventually, I climbed down some very steep and large stone steps, which was not easy for my short legs, to the lowest level and sought out someone in a uniform. I told the person that I was separated from my group. Two people took me to an exit area where there were more guards. Apparently I had been reported missing, so they knew where to send me. Everyone was relieved to see me again. But I hadn't been concerned at all. I never felt unsafe the entire time I was in India.

Our group was the last to leave the fort. We piled into the SUV and began a long drive back to Delhi. But first we stopped in Rajasthan to do some shopping in a large building that housed a variety of areas where one could buy anything from carpets to jewelry. Now, that was a great shopping spree!

I purchased a lot of things from a jeweler to resell at my salon and some curtains that I would find a place for in my home. It was quite dark by the time we left, probably around seven or eight o'clock. We drove from there for hours before we stopped to eat at a roadside touristy place. Just quick sandwiches were what we had and then off we went again for hours.

During this time I had a lot of opportunity to talk with Lakshman since we were the two seated in the very back. Basically, he gave me satsang in answer to my questions. I expressed to him some of my not-so-great qualities that I wanted to change. He told me that we can't correct anything unless we first recognize it. So I had taken the first step by recognizing areas that needed correction.

Lakshman spoke about remaining calm at all times. Chaos may be all around us, but we should see ourselves like the hub of a wheel. We must endeavor to stay in the hub where it is peaceful and calm. The answers are not in the outer world, outside of ourselves, they are within. We should keep returning to the center, the wheel hub, where we will always find peace.

I asked about the difficulty of focusing on the breath when so many thoughts are determined to disturb my concentration. Lakshman said that it does get easier as one practices. We must surrender to the process and just let go. Everyone has problems with this area, so I am normal. When thoughts creep in, gently push them aside and return to the focus. Over and over again, if necessary.

I had this idea that it might be fun to offer mehandi art at my salon. Since I'm an artist, I thought I could give women henna tattoos. I asked Lakshman about purchasing the equipment and he said he would handle it for me.

Eventually we arrived back at the Guatam Hotel in Delhi. I think it was one in the morning. We all retired to our rooms and waited for our stored luggage to be brought upstairs to us. This time I was in a room across from Dr. T. Tim and Albert had their same room. I collapsed into bed, totally rung out from the trip. So much driving in such a few days, who wouldn't be totally exhausted?

We all rose late and tottered down to eat breakfast around ten or eleven. I think the original plan had been to leave the hotel around noon, but it turned out to be more like two. Lakshman gathered us from the lobby where we had been waiting. We were then taken to the ashram in Delhi. My three guys were going to be staying there and I was leaving that evening, although I was given a wonderful room. I could have happily remained in that room for weeks! Besides the two king beds, there was a table with an altar. A glorious framed picture of Maharaj Ji dressed in vibrant orange looked back at me. I fell in love with the picture. On either side was a framed picture of his parents, along with some incense and a candle. The bathroom was large and typical of others I had seen in the ashrams.

We were served lunch in a large room that was outside of the quarters the guys were given to stay. We met several Bai Jis and other staff members. One of the Bai Jis gave me a tour of the ashram. This also gave me the opportunity to make a donation for my accommodations at Prem Nagar. We were never charged for any meals or for the rooms while we stayed there. We only paid for the vehicle rentals, which was very inexpensive. The generosity was unbelievable, so I gladly made a cash donation.

We were able to shop at the ashram, so I eagerly purchased a copy of the picture of Maharaj Ji that I loved featured in my room and some other items. While waiting for time to pass before I would be driven to the airport, I used the table in my room to finish up some notes in my journal so I wouldn't forget one precious moment of this transformational adventure. Someone knocked on my door and it turned out to be a nice woman who had been sent by Lakshman to purchase the supplies necessary to perform mehandi art. She was a mehandi artist. I paid her in rupees and thanked her. Then Albert came to visit, so I practiced using the clay paint on his arm. Ah, more practice needed!

Just before I left, some of us were gathered on the porch outside my room. Lakshman appeared to present me with a gift from Mata Ji. It was a lovely lavender scarf to use during meditation. And it was the perfect color! I was so surprised and delighted at her thoughtfulness and just the mere fact she even knew I was leaving today.

My time was ending in Delhi and transportation was arranged for me to get to the airport. Unfortunately, I was the only one leaving. The others had two more weeks, although each one had at one time expressed that they wished they had planned to stay just two weeks. I figured after they saw Katmandu and Nepal, no one would be sorry to have stayed longer than me. But I couldn't justify staying a total of four weeks away from my business, so, here I was about to depart alone from a foreign country out of a strange airport.

Tim and a Bai Ji accompanied me to the airport. Tim and I said goodbye and I stepped alone inside this giant airport, not having a clue where to go first. My thought was, I can always ask questions, I can't be the only person who has ever been in this situation and, so, I asked questions. I stopped one man to ask where Continental was located because the sign just had an arrow and I was way past the pointed direction.

I finally located the airline and everything went as smooth as one could expect. Over all, it was a very pleasant flight, coming and going, especially considering I had never traveled overseas or experienced a trip through Customs. Keeping paperwork together to present to someone was not hard, and customs was a breeze for me. I guess I didn't look like a terrorist with my red hair. Yes, there were some long lines, but, hey, there were a lot of people on both planes. Common sense would tell someone it would take a bit of time to go through the lines.

I arrived safely back at the Orlando Airport, on time and very happy.

The Word in its primordial stage existed as the soul of life of God.
Shri Satpal Ji Maharaj

Chapter Six
Satsang

A satsang is a spiritual discourse. This is my satsang to you.

Life is all about experiencing God. People will tell you there are many paths to God, and I would agree. But I am advocating Knowledge. The three key principles of Knowledge are controlling the mind, being in the present moment and love. We'll start with the mind.

The mind is a control freak. It wants to dictate everything we think, feel, believe and express. Knowledge teaches us that we must take back control of the mind and make it obey our true self. That is much easier said than done.

Have you ever tried not to think about something? And what happens? That's all we can think about. The mind is stubborn and wants to wield its will, not listen to what we want. Besides, if it were to allow us to control it, what would happen? It wouldn't be in control anymore! Heaven forbid our minds would not be in control! You see, it's all about that arrogant pipsqueak ego that keeps us under control. It is the ego that is dictating to us, being resistant to change. And change is exactly what we need to do in order to achieve happiness,

Everyone I think I have ever spoken to about meditation has declared how difficult it is to focus. In other words, our minds won't allow us to focus. It keeps sending in thoughts about paying the water bill, how horribly John is behaving at work, why the teacher is picking on little Billie and so forth. We are barraged by useless thoughts that merely distract us from our goal.

Have you ever taken an exam and all you can think about is something totally disconnected from the exam?

Here is an important moment, and the mind is sending in thoughts about some silly matter that isn't going to gain you a decent grade or a promotion. The mind has no consideration, it only wants to behave like a spoiled child.

As parents, when a child is acting spoiled by throwing a temper tantrum, what do we do? At first we might ignore the situation because that's what the experts tell us to do. But after the situation has calmed down, we endeavor to bring this poor behavior to an end. We take control.

As adult human beings, we display spoiled behaviors as much as children. We demand our way, throwing tantrums, perhaps not in the middle of a department store, but still, we permit a full blown rage to enter into a relationship. We want it our way! Not your way or his way, but MY way! The ego is making a statement in the ugliest manner possible. But we can't allow ourselves to behave this way. We can't be acting in a manner that is destructive to others, not to mention, ourselves. We have to take control of our bad behaviors, our bratty egos.

This is not an easy task. I believe it is one we will be working on for the rest of our days. The ego does not go down gently. Learning to control the mind is like trying to stop a train that has already left the station. This mind has been in control for however many years we have been existing on the earth. It isn't going to happen overnight that suddenly it will relinquish its hold. As with anything else in life worth achieving, it takes practice.

When negative thoughts come into our minds, we have to first recognize that they exist and then change the thought to a positive one. This takes awareness of the moment, being present. We must first be aware of what we are thinking, how we are behaving, what plan we are hatching and so forth in order to recognize when we are stepping out of bounds. When we recognize our missteps, we then are in a position to correct. We change our thinking.

Suppose we are always thinking unkind thoughts about a particular person at work. We don't like this person and find him or her to be obnoxious. So, a negative thought jumps in and we become aware of its existence. That is the first opportunity that we are given to change the thought pattern. We attempt to look at this person with nonjudgmental eyes. That's a positive start. Why is this person acting in such a manner? Perhaps she or he is lonely, we suspect, because there is not a relationship in this person's life. Recently this person has gained weight, distancing the possibility of a relationship even further. This adds unhappiness to the scenario. What else could be happening in his or her life that we know nothing about? It could be anything imaginable.

In this way we start to see this person through compassion rather than distaste. Our changed view may not make any difference in the person's life, although it might, but it will make a significant difference in our lives. The reason is, we have chosen to see this person differently, with compassion, so the next time she or he behaves badly, we understand and can ignore the behavior. We do not allow ourselves to get agitated, we remain calm and understanding. That's a big change from our previous behavior around this person. We were in the moment through awareness, took control of our reactions and responded with love. After all, we can't change the situation, but we can change how we perceive it and respond.

Awareness works equally well when we are allowing our ego to get out of control. Once we start recognizing when we are acting from a point of ego, we can do something about it. I have become better at recognizing that I am about to say something inappropriate, so I often catch myself before the inappropriate thought flies out of my mouth. I realize it will be an egotistical remark or is being said to promote myself as superior or some other equally incorrect act. At the point of recognition, I stop the remark and change it around or eliminate it altogether.

By continually being aware—being in the moment--of our reactions and actions, we learn to control our mind in a positive way. All this will serve a purpose when we are trying to meditate and all those wild thoughts come barging into the peace we had hoped to attain.

During meditation, the ego mind desperately wants to take control. It does not want us to be independent. It does not want us to be liberated from control. So we must be diligent in our pursuit to control our minds. If the mind sways away from our objective, we simply must keep bringing it back to our focus. Over and over and over again. And that is quite normal. We are human beings, not saints. We must keep practicing until we get to the Carnegie Hall of perfection.

When we go shopping at a mall or to a county fair with our young children, they hold onto our hands. The tiny hand clasps tightly around a finger or two, keeping that protective connection to the parent. Should the child lose contact with the parent, he or she would be lost, unprotected. It is the same with regard to our connection to God. If we lose connection, we are lost and not within that loving embrace. It is through meditation that we make our connection to God. That is why it is so important to meditate, to keep that connection open to God.

Knowledge shows us how to bridge that perceived divide between us and God because God is always with us anyway, whether we realize it or not. God does not disconnect from us, rather, it is us who disconnect from God. But it is in that realization that we gain the peace and love we seek, and that is done through meditation. So by focusing ourselves onto the present moment and controlling our minds we are able to focus more clearly in our meditations, which opens us all up to realizing peace and love. That wonderful eternal bliss.

Love is always the answer to any dilemma. When we touch into the love that God has for us, we feel "joyed up" as I like to say. We can feel the love inside our chests and we are so full to the brim that our love spills out to others. And that's a good thing! There can never be too much love. As corny as it may sound, if we could ALL just love each other there would never be another war. Families would function as connective members, businesses would be rid of egotistical behaviors and greed, politicians would truly work for their constituent's benefit and everyone would care lovingly for the earth. And that starts with each one of us. If one person endeavors to love more, another will be affected by that love. The second person will respond with love and affect another, and so on.......

There is hope for this world we live in. And that hope begins with YOU.

It is only by meditation on the Word that the form of God, that is, Light, is seen and the cosmic form of God realized.
Tulsida, mystic poet and saint

Chapter Seven
I'm Home, Now What?

When we returned from India, we had to acclimate ourselves into the normalcy of life as we know it here in the United States. The entire time over there, our minds were not concerned about bills, jobs, family and the daily stresses of life. Our focus was clearly on the spiritual activities of meditation, learning and growing. Some of us had an easy time adjusting and some of us didn't.

Albert kept right on seeking and growing spiritually. Since he lives alone, he was able to control his environment, which helped to keep the flow going. He went onto accept a job as a medical caretaker, thus giving service to others. Albert meshed his former spiritual practices with the new ones, settling into a comfortable spiritual existence.

Dr. T returned home a bit more reserved, sort of keeping close his experiences. He also was inspired to open a metaphysical center. In past years, Dr. T had operated a successful center in California and felt led to do so again, this time in Florida. He now offers church services that are a blend of Christianity and Spiritualism, development classes and seminars to the public. At the time of this writing, his center will be hosting Shri Vibhu Ji Maharaj when he visits our area for one week.

Tim extended his stay in India ten days after Albert and Dr. T departed. During this time he was privileged to stay at the residence of Shri Satpal Ji Maharaj and spent a great deal of time in meditation. When Tim returned it was difficult for him to acclimate back into his world. For about two weeks after his return, he sequestered himself in his motor home at a park in St. Augustine, Florida, in an attempt to keep India close. He also chose to separate himself from his three traveling buddies and those who traveled to India the previous year. Tim did not take phone calls from any of his friends and was even a bit standoffish around his wife.

Although my feelings were hurt because I couldn't contact him, I imagined that this had been such a profound experience for him that his heart and soul were still in India and wanted to remain there forever. But Tim had obligations. It must have been very stressful to be torn between the spiritual euphoria he felt and the reality we know to be life in this materialistic world we all live in.

My adjustment to my new life went fairly well, considering my environment. I am not in a situation like Albert is where I can control my environment. My mother-in-law lives with my husband and me and she lacks interest or involvement in anything spiritual. That's not conducive to my spiritual growth. But my husband is open to my new beliefs and practices, especially since we met in the Cassadaga Spiritualist Camp. Neither one of us is a traditional thinker, otherwise we wouldn't have wound up in Cassadaga with a bunch of Spiritualists!

I have come to realize that my mother-in-law is a teacher. She is here in my home to present me with opportunities for growth. Coming from a different generation and being brought up in an environment entirely different than I was has created two people who don't view things the same way. We are very different people.

The good part is, she isn't like my mother, who used to yell at me all the time when she was alive. She never yells at me and she is quite generous, so I could have it much worse! But because of our differences, she gives me opportunities to adjust my thinking so I can see her in a compassionate light and with understanding. It's the least I can do to make her last days tolerable, despite her illnesses. So, I ask consistently for patience and strength from God.

I find myself rethinking situations and responding to incidents at work and elsewhere more slowly by observing what's happening first. I try to step back so I can "witness my emotions." This helps me to better myself spiritually so I don't let something inappropriate fly out of my mouth. Other times it's my ego flaunting itself and I have to endeavor to recognize that situation as much as possible so I can squelch it. Witnessing the emotions we feel daily is so important for our spiritual growth. When we learn to understand why we feel a certain way and then react inappropriately, we can bring our less-than-positive tendencies under control before they cause damage.

The area that is giving me the most problem is the meditation. As I've always said, with no practical experience until now, it's easier to be spiritual when meditating on top of a mountain than when involved in our material world. How true is that statement! During meditation in India, there were no rude thoughts invading my peace. Once at home, all those invaders came pouring in at warp speed. I am bombarded by my daily grind, stresses and concerns, pelting my consciousness with distracting thoughts. It is so difficult to turn that off and focus.

I am fortunate to have Helen to email and call for suggestions. Helen also supplied me with cell numbers so I could talk with a Mahatma or Bai Ji. Audrey in New York also is only a phone call away, eager to help anyway she can. Every conversation with her is like receiving satsang.

My morning meditations sometimes are vague because I am still sleepy. It is so easy to curl up and go back to sleep—and sometimes I do! That feeling does not help my meditation. The evening meditations are better and more constructive. I discovered that when I meditate after a day where I am happy that my meditations are better. During those times, I physically feel the love inside me. I concluded that when I meditate with that feeling of love in my heart, my meditations are successful. How simple, the answer is love! Well, isn't love always the answer to any situation?

Some nights I am so "joyed up" after meditation that I can't settle down to sleep. It is like I am happy, happy with my life and feeling blissful. I go through periods where meditation is very good, followed by periods where it is difficult. One thing I have discovered is, I think we all make this meditation far more difficult than it truly is. I believe if we can stop fighting the meditation and just learn to surrender into our breath, our meditations will improve. At least this has worked for me—when I can surrender.

At one point after my return, meditation was really tough, before I discovered how easy it is to surrender to the experience. I hadn't had satsang in so long and felt like I had lost something of substance that I had gained in India. Like that something had dribbled away from a once full puddle with promise to a trickle from a faucet that clearly is a maybe. I felt like I was here alone. My meditations were so busy with intruding thoughts about everything in my external life that I had lost focus. Everyone who I asked said that focusing is the most difficult thing to do. So, I guess that makes me normal. But I needed satsang!

At that time the holidays were approaching, just a week shy of Christmas. The grocery was brimming with tempting cookies, clients were bringing in trays of goodies for us at the salon, which I devoured, and I was overeating at night, I believe, out of boredom. I guess I was trying to fill the vacancy inside with food, a vacancy that can only be filled with satsang. I needed to get a grip on myself, but I didn't seem to have the desire at that moment to turn me around.

Where were those lifetime buddies I traveled to India with, I wondered? Then again, it was unfair to throw that responsibility on any of them. We each have to find our own way and muster the strength to be dedicated. Dedication. That was what I was lacking. At that time I was still meditating twice daily, but not with quality. I was getting lazy because this was work. Once we receive Knowledge, our devotion and dedication doesn't end, as if to suggest that we have it all now. I began to realize that I was lacking discipline, as Vibhu Ji spoke about during the satsang he delivered in Prem Nagar. I placed blame on not being inspired through satsang. I felt I needed sustenance to nourish my spirit, some nectar to quench my thirst. My only satsang came through the monthly magazine the society publishes, but it wasn't the same as when one sits in the presence of Maharaj Ji, a Mahatma or a Bai Ji.

It was about this time that I received word from Helen that Mahatma Gargi Bai Ji was in Florida and eventually would be traveling to the Orlando area. She wanted to meet with some Premies, so Helen encouraged me to call her. And I did. This was exactly what I needed to rekindle the spark of dedication.

In December, just after Christmas, ten of us met at an Indian woman's house on the outskirts of Orlando. Gargi Bai Ji asked Tim to talk about his trip to India. I was asked to speak about my experience and then Don, who is part of the group that traveled to India the year before, gave his rendition of his experience. Liz spoke briefly about how India had affected her as well. A delicious Indian lunch was served, followed by picture taking and chatting.

At one point Tim and I were able to talk privately outside for the first time since his return. He confirmed how profound his experience had been and why he was separating himself from others. It all made sense now. I was very relieved because I cherish the friendships of these three men I shared the spiritual experience of a lifetime with on our journey. Thereafter, all our relationships with Tim returned to normal.

Mahatma Gargi Bai Ji is an inspiring woman of sixty years, very tiny and so very sweet. She told us the story of how she came to be a Bai Ji. She had always wanted to know God and had been raised with scripture, so she knew it well, but it didn't answer her questions. She eventually met numerous gurus who still didn't give her the answers she sought. Some suggested mantras, but she had repeated mantras since childhood and still had not seen God, so she knew that wasn't the way. Eventually she came to hear of Knowledge from Shri Hans Ji Maharaj. She knew this was what she had been looking for all her young life. After receiving Knowledge, she said she was "out of this world" for three days. Gargi Bai Ji was nineteen at the time.

Gargi Bai Ji and Patches at Tim and Liz's home.

Shri Sagat Mata Ji, the wife of Shri Hans Ji Maharaj, asked her to come live at her ashram, which surprised Gargi Bai Ji. Why me, she questioned? I just received Knowledge. But she accepted the invitation. From that time forward, she was privileged to be present for many exciting events, such as the marriage of the holy couple's son, Shri Satpal Ji Maharaj, and hold Vibhu Ji, his son, as a babe.

Gargi Bai Ji is one of the front people who go ahead of Maharaj Ji and Vibhu Ji, speaking of Knowledge so when they come the people will be prepared to receive Knowledge. She also resides at ashrams when there is a need for satsang in that community. The Indian lady who was offering her home for the satsang had been initiated sixteen years prior and had received Knowledge from Gargi Bai Ji in South Florida.

When we were leaving, I was so pleased to be able to bow to her and touch her feet. She tried to suggest by a wave of her hand that I didn't need to do this, but I dropped to my knees, touched her feet with my hands and said, this is a privilege and I have wanted to do this for a long time since coming back from India. I then placed my forehead on her feet with great joy.

When she stood up I realized she was my height. I remarked how tiny she is and she asked for Liz to take a picture of us. She said I was sweet when I said she was sweet. Such a wonderful Bai Ji!

After we left, I felt all joyed-up, like I had a buzz on. That feeling continued for two days. It was wonderful to feel that way again. Ah, the joy one experiences when being in the presence of Mahatmas and Bai Jis!

Since returning home from India, I have adjusted my thinking and discovered what works for me. We are all individuals and what works for one doesn't necessarily work for another. Sometimes it takes patience and experimentation to finally discover what we personally need/require to get it right for our personalities and environments. One size does not fit all! For some it will take longer than others. But time is not the important element. Everything happens when it is supposed to and at the perfect time.

Often if a practice is too easy, we don't appreciate its value and dismiss it. Sort of like, if it doesn't cost a lot, it can't have much worth. But that isn't true. Simple is often the way to go. Sometimes something is so natural that it's easy. We just have to let go and flow to receive the beauty of the experience.

I have continued to be vegetarian with no difficulty and am having fun experimenting with Indian cuisine and visiting Indian groceries in Orlando for all the ingredients I need to prepare the dishes. My husband and I both adore Indian food, but my mother-in-law isn't so keen on it. I have to adjust the temperature of the spices so it isn't too hot for her to handle. Sometimes she remarks that a dish tastes strange. Obviously, they didn't have Indian restaurants in her day up in New Hampshire. She's a meat and potatoes kind of person, so I cook my husband and her meat and a vegetarian dish and I eat only the vegetarian part. Other nights I make a vegetarian meal for everyone.

***

Tim, Dr. T, Albert and I came to India seeking Knowledge, and like the group that traveled from Cassadaga the year before, we received it. This *Knowledge* is about experiencing our personal divinity; it's about self-discovery, self-mastery and the dedicated effort to remain, to use a common term, centered. To be in balance, an observer of what's happening, so we are *present*. Only through that conscious presence can we understand the world and experience our true selves being revealed to us. We are able to see the world as a manifestation of God's creative energy. It's all God in disguise.

So, that's pretty simple: we're all one and God lives within each of us and everything else. The trick is to *live* from that perspective every waking moment. It's probably impossible, unless you're a saint. That's why in India it is a given that we need a teacher, a guru, to guide us.

I continue to meditate daily and am strong in my love. Shri Vibhu Ji is coming soon and we will be privileged to receive many satsangs from him. I am so excited over this opportunity for spiritual growth!

One of the greatest philosophies of spirituality teaches us that we are complete in ourselves, it is just that we do not know it.
Shri Vibhu Ji Maharaj

Chapter Eight
Shri Vibhu Ji is Here!

Shri Vibhu Ji Maharaj arrived Friday evening and six of us were at the airport to greet him at the beginning of the Memorial Day weekend. Prior to his arrival, Liz and I had driven down to Tampa to pick up Gargi Bai Ji from the ashram. Both of them would be staying at Tim and Liz's house during Vibhu Ji's visit. Gargi Bai would be cooking Indian dishes for Vibhu Ji and any of us fortunate enough to be present to enjoy her delicious cuisine.

After Vibhu Ji had settled into the couch, I asked him about his trip and if his parents had returned from their European tour with one hundred Premies? He asked me about my manuscript for this book and said he would like to read it. I was delighted and said I would bring him a copy tomorrow.

Saturday a group gathered for a scheduled satsang at Dr. T's metaphysical center. It was so wonderful to hear Vibhu Ji's voice delivering satsang again. Everything had come full circle from last year when I first heard him speak and fell in love with his spiritual energy. However, this time I knew more and could appreciate his wisdom more thoroughly having been to India. Not that everyone has to travel to India, but for me it expanded my appreciation and understanding.

After the program was over, I told Vibhu Ji that I had my manuscript in my car, and did he want me to give it to Liz? He said he would come with me. Once outside, people wanted to talk to him, so I walked around the next building to where my car was parked. There certainly was no need for him to follow me, I would retrieve the manuscript and bring it to him. As I turned around from the car, I saw Vibhu walking over to me, much to my surprise. I told him he didn't have to do that, but he insisted it was all right. I gave him my manuscript and said if there were any glaring inaccuracies, to please mark it as such. Then he turned and walked back around the building to the others.

I drove out of the parking lot and became so overcome with emotion, I began to cry. This wasn't a normal tears-running-down-the-cheek kind of cry, I sobbed for at least half the distance home. I was so privileged to have Shri Vibhu Ji read my manuscript, I guess I just overflowed with gratitude and appreciation. And maybe I also needed a cleansing.

Sunday I went to the Lyceum Service in Cassadaga where Vibhu Ji was speaking. As soon as I entered the door, Vibhu Ji greeted me and spoke about my book. He had read half way through and said he was enjoying it. That was very pleasing news!

`After he gave satsang to a room filled with people, we all adjourned to walk down to the church. By the time the service started, almost every seat was taken. The members of the two groups who traveled to India in 2008 and 2009 who became Premies were seated in the front row. We each were given several stems of white roses and were asked to line up against the wall beside the stage. Margarita led the procession by placing a garland around Shri Vibhu Ji's neck and gave him her roses. The rest of us followed, presenting him with roses and bowing. As an introduction for Vibhu Ji, Don, who was chairing the service, introduced each of us Premies, stating when we went to India and some small individual detail. Next, we were once again blessed with satsang.

Liz and I collected Vibhu Ji from the crowd of admirers to take him back to the house for lunch. Gargi Bai had prepared a wonderful meal of spicy dal, rice, rotis, spicy potatoes and very hot okra. Liz and I were in heaven! I brought a pudding for dessert.

Shri Vibhu Ji ate first and alone in the dining room and we ate in the great room where the kitchen is located. A special aluminum plate is used for his meals along with several small aluminum cups for chutneys and other things, an aluminum drinking cup and utensils. After he ate, Gargi Bai told me to clean his dishes and then said that it was an honor to do so. I sensed that it was an honor and I did feel honored as I carefully washed each piece of dinnerware, enjoying every precious moment. I placed all the small cups, drinking cup and silverware I had washed on top of the plate and returned all the dinnerware to the dining room table for future use.

Liz and Gargi Bai left to shop for groceries, so Albert and I talked at the table. All of a sudden Vibhu Ji appeared before us, holding my manuscript. He said to me that he had finished my book and it was very good, then he gave me some suggestions about bringing more spirituality into it. I had been so afraid to divulge anything we had vowed to keep secret that I had left out certain things. After he literally gave me a private satsang for thirty minutes, I felt relieved and more confident about what I could speak about. I assured him I would go back through the book and add more experiences now that I better understood what I could share.

We returned to Cassadaga for the scheduled 3:00 p.m. satsang, which was very well attended. Every time I hear satsang, I take away another special experience and learn something new. By this time I'm sure I wasn't the only one wishing Vibhu Ji would stay with us permanently. He is such a blessing to have with us and our love and devotion just grows bigger and brighter every second we are with him.

Again, we returned to Tim and Liz's house and ate more food. Oh, am I going to miss Gargi Bai's cooking after she leaves! She has promised to teach Liz and me to cook on a girl's weekend at the Tampa ashram. I can't wait to learn Indian cooking from an expert!

I had heard so much about a man named Sam who lives in California who has been a devotee and Premie for thirty-five or more years. He has filmed many satsangs through his production company and was coming to Florida to participate in the satsangs that Vibhu Ji was giving. And now he has arrived to stay with Tim and Liz.

Sam, Albert and Tim were doing the guy-thing outside in Tim's "Chai tent" when Liz and I decided to pay a visit. The atmosphere that Tim has created in the Chai tent is quite nice. Besides the Buddha, there is an altar with a dozen tiny Buddhas and many pictures of the entire holy family. It's quite comfortable and a good place for the men to talk while lounging in the chairs, sipping tea.

Vibhu Ji had been invited to go to Don's house, so several of the men scurried off. Liz and I were not going because we had had a long day after a previously long day. I was going home.

Monday evening we all met at Dr. T's center again for satsang and would do the same on Tuesday and Wednesday as well. And so the joy just kept on lowing.....We were so blessed!

Shri Vibhu Ji Maharaj

As much as we enjoyed Vibhu Ji being with us, I believe he enjoyed himself equally as much. Last year he had expressed an interest in spending some time in St. Augustine, so this year Tim made sure his wish came true. Being a lover of history, Vibhu Ji truly appreciated the experience of visiting the oldest continuously occupied European-established city and the oldest port in the continental United States.

On Memorial Day, Albert organized a picnic at a park where everyone could go canoeing and biking--and Vibhu Ji himself went for a bike ride. One just doesn't imagine a member of the holy family riding a bike. The American tradition of corn on the cob and watermelon were enjoyed by Vibhu Ji on this special holiday. Then, much to the amazement of everyone, Vibhu Ji participated in a game of volleyball! He rolled up his long, white shirt sleeves and had a great time slapping the ball over the net.

A couple days later, Vibhu Ji visited Blue Spring State Park, although the famous manatees were not there at that time of year. He even went for a swim in the icy cold waters of the spring. Slowly, slowly, he inched into the water until he could no longer delay the ultimate chilling impact of being totally immersed in the frigid water. Later that night he joked during satsang about the experience.

Early Thursday morning, his last day with all of us, Vibhu Ji gave a special satsang to Premies at Tim and Liz's house. It was so wonderful to hear him speak of Knowledge and answer questions. He emphasized that focusing on our breath during meditation is where the journey begins. It does no good to receive Knowledge unless we put into practice the proper ways to live. Vibhu Ji said that when we meditate we take one step forward, but if we then follow that meditation by acting badly towards another, we take one step backwards. Even if we read scripture, attend satsang and meditate, we will not advance spiritually unless we put into practice the teachings.

He advised us to act with purity of heart and that if

we do, our lives will change. Vibhu Ji spoke about how when we get mad or act selfishly, for example, we should tell ourselves that we are not that bad behavior. We are so much more. That divine spark of God that dwells inside each of us is who we truly are, a shining spirit, a beautiful soul. We must endeavor to reflect our pure interior outward to all.

Vibhu Ji also reviewed with us the proper way to meditate. Having a straight spine is very important while we sit with our legs folded inward, yoga style. This is a beneficial position because the body will form a pyramid. A pyramid formation attracts cosmic energy to us. It is important to lock the spiritual energy within by closing any area where energy can escape, such as through our hands and/or feet. If we were to sit, for instance, with our legs placed straight out from us, our feet would allow energy to escape through the soles. So rather than let that occur, we are to cross our legs inward in the yogic fashion.

As for the hands, he suggested that we fold our hands or place one hand over the other with the palms facing upward or touch the thumb on each hand to the index finger, forming a circle, with the two hands resting in the lap.

The perfect time to meditate is between four and six o'clock in the morning. Realizing in the West that we may not wish to rise so early or have to rush to work, Vibhu Ji said that this was the ideal time, but not mandatory. Given our busy lives, he acknowledged that we may not be able to meditate for an hour at a time. He suggested that the most important element is that we meditate, even if it's for only ten minutes. When we have more time, we can meditate for a longer period.

Eight of us then drove to DeLeon Springs State Park where we were treated to pancakes that we made ourselves on the grill built into the table at this quaint, old restaurant. Our dear Shri Vibhu Ji Maharaj had fun flipping pancakes and eating them. As I've said so many times, he is the real deal. There is no pretense with this spiritual teacher.

We all went our separate ways in the parking lot. Tim and Liz will take Vibhu Ji and Gargi Bai to Tampa where Vibhu Ji will deliver a couple programs. Then he and Gargi Bai are off to Vancouver, California, Mexico, Texas, Pennsylvania and New York before he flies to England for yet another program.

The joy I felt throughout Shri Vibhu Ji Maharaj's visit with us has carried through to this day and I believe this wonderful energy will remain as I carry a piece of him within my heart forever. We have all been so blessed. Ah, the joy one feels when in the company of Saints!

I have noticed a change in my meditations and my attitude since Vibhu Ji has departed. Sometimes in the past, I must admit, I have felt obligated to meditate. But now I am eager to meditate! I look forward to the experience, no matter what it may be that evening. I try not to "expect" anything, just to live in the moment.

While my meditations have improved because my dedication is present, that doesn't mean there is a light show every night. Meditation does vary from one time to the next. I think that helps us from expecting or feeling entitled to see or hear. Knowledge teaches us to be desireless. That is, performing a task without expecting a particular result. We do an action for the sake of the action rather than the anticipation of the outcome. Each day I endeavor to be desireless and this helps my meditations.

***

Every day, I very much miss being at Prem Nagar Ashram, my spiritual home. I miss being in the presence of Satguru Shri Satpal Ji Maharaj, in the company of Shri Vibhu Ji Maharaj and Mahatma Ji Fakiranand and all the other lovely, loving people at the ashram.

I am eternally grateful for the experience of a lifetime I witnessed there and all the blessings I have received from Maharaj Ji. Through the grace of Satguru

Shri Satpal Ji Maharaj, I have been given Knowledge, which is the greatest of gifts that anyone can attain. In a manner of speaking, he placed me on a path and said, "The rest is up to you. Now it's your turn to walk."

So I am walking daily. I take care of the temple that houses the life force within. I meditate to know God. I am amending behaviors and thoughts, and I more regularly practice gratitude so I may live a more peaceful existence. I feel to be worthy of this most precious gift, I must do my part each day. So I walk. And I will keep on walking until my day has ended.

………..In the future I will do a sequel to this book as I become more familiar with Knowledge and able to share how it has affected my life, God willing, of course………..

Acknowledgements

I am very grateful for the critiquing and encouragement that I received from Helen Clapham regarding the creation of this book. Helen is a true soul sister and a divine human being.

My soul sister, Liz Williams, who has the kindest heart on the planet and sets the bar for giving of herself. I am grateful that we have been brought together. She is family.

And then there is Audrey Fowler who has kept me inspired. Her telephone satsangs have pulled me through when I needed clarity. Another soul sister.

I am truly blessed knowing these remarkable women.

APPENDIX

Packing for India

I found the book *A Lonely Planet: India* to be very helpful with its recommendations about clothing, shopping, restaurants, hotels and everything in general. I heeded all the precautions and I think I was very prepared. I encouraged everyone in our group to use antibacterial liquid gel on the planes and trains and hand wipes for the bathrooms, all of which I carried. I handed out all the above to anyone in my party who was willing to follow my advice. I was the most diligent one. As a result, I was the only one who didn't contract a cold.

The cardinal rule is, don't drink the water. Only drink from sealed water bottles, which are prevalent there. Ice is also off limits, so use caution in restaurants. Most everywhere I went, the food was vegetarian. But after I left India, the guys found places to eat pizza and burgers. So if you have a craving for a burger, that can be found in some towns, even Kentucky Fried Chicken!

I brought more cash than traveler's checks, which is a personal choice. I hid money in my ticket/passport holder that is worn around the neck for convenience at the airport, a small black purse that could be worn strapped around my waist and in a money belt. The money belt at any one time usually held the most money because it was easily concealed under all my blouses or shirts. Once I left the airport scene, the money in my ticket/passport holder went into my purse. I knew from traveling in New York City, it's best to have money and credit cards hidden in several places, even several locations within my purse. We also were able to place cash in a central safe at the Hotel Guatum or one within our rooms, depending where we were staying at the time.

Someone did try to lift Tim's wallet from his back pocket. Fortunately, he hadn't placed it there. Men should never carry a wallet in their back pocket when in big cities or foreign countries. It's much too easy for a pickpocket to steal.

Some things are ridiculously inexpensive to purchase in India. For little money, one can purchase some impressive Christmas gifts and wonderful personal items. Come prepared to spend money.

It is probably a good idea to carry two bags with one being considerably smaller. This will be more convenient if you want to do a couple quick stopovers. Hauling around a large suitcase is not going to be much fun in the crowded streets of a big city. Think Spartan when traveling and staying in ashrams. The simpler the better.

The weather in India is mostly hot, although it does vary from region to region. During certain times of the year, like March into June, temperatures can reach anywhere from one hundred to one hundred and fifteen and then add onto that the dust blowing around. You are going to sweat a lot! Be prepared to wear cool cottons and do not bring synthetic fabrics. You'll just be too hot. Carry a hand fan so you can whip up a breeze for yourself.

It's still very warm in September, but usually only in the nineties. The temperature starts dropping after that until it can become chilly at night beginning around December. In March it starts the warm up trend again. From June through September, and even October in some regions, is monsoon season where it rains for days at a time. Not the best time to go to India.

Here are some items that you would be wise to carry:

> Change your currency into Rupees. The approximate exchange for an American ten dollar bill is 471.031 Rupees.
> Bring a Visa or Master Card.
> Prescription medications: bring double in case of theft.
> Plastic baggies
> Camera

Passport holder

An adapter for the foreign electrical outlets to charge your cell phone and batteries and so you can use a blowdryer or other such appliance

Antibacterial cream, antifungal cream, insect repellant, diarrhea stopper, anti-nausea medication, antihistamine, Dramamine, Hydrocortizone cream, Ibuprophen and a laxative.

Sunscreen

Umbrella

Hat

Hand fan

Band aids

Safety pins

Personal items like a hairbrush, toothbrush, makeup, small mirror, shave cream, and razor for shaving face or legs.

Bath towel and wash cloth in case you are staying at an ashram that doesn't provide such. Plan to leave them behind for someone else to use who didn't think to bring towels. This will also allow room for purchases in your suitcase.

And the most important thing of all—Toilet Paper! I brought two rolls just in case there was a shortage. As it turned out, I gave a roll away to one of my traveling companions who stayed longer.

I brought some old underwear and tossed it before I left the ashram or hotel, depending where I was at the time. I had bought a skirt at Goodwill just for this trip and I left it in the hotel over a chair. My thought was the maid could take it for herself if she wanted. This action has the benefit of making extra room for some purchases in your suitcase.

Glossary

Arti: this is a very ancient ritual hymn. This hymn is also adapted to praising one's spiritual Master.

Ashram: a building or compound where a guru lives and teaches spirituality.

Bai Ji: female version of a Mahatma. One who teaches the spiritual truths and transfers the grace from Maharaj Ji of Knowledge to the initiate. Bai Ji is similar to a nun. Sometimes seen as Baiji or baiji. Proper example would be Mahatma Gargi Bai Ji.

Chakra: a Sanskrit word referring to seven major energy centers (also understood as wheels of light) that are generally believed to exist within the subtle body. These energy centers are located along the spine.

Chapati: an Indian flat bread.

Dal: a dish served often at every meal that is comprised of lentils or other beans. This is a mainstay in the Indian culture.

Devotee: one who is devoted to the spiritual master.

Ghat: swimming area.

Guru: teacher. This is a Sanskrit word. Gu means darkness, ru means light; one who leads us from darkness into light.

Ji: term of respect.

Mahatma: great soul. Maha means great; atman means soul. a male who teaches the spiritual truths and bestows the grace from Maharaj Ji of Knowledge to the initiate.

Mata: mother. Mata Ji is a term of respect for one's mother or for an older woman. In this book the reference is Spiritual Mother. Therefore, the wife of a guru is Mata Ji.

Premie: a term used to describe those who have been initiated into Knowledge.

Roti: a flat bread made with whole wheat and other grains that is frequently served at meals.

Satguru: true guru; guru of gurus.

Satsang: a spiritual discourse.

Shri: a prefix, such as mister, to enhance another title, such as Shri Satpal Ji Maharaj.

Additional Books Written by Elizabeth Owens

How To Communicate With Spirits

Spiritualism and Clairvoyance for Beginners

Discover Your Spiritual Life

Women Celebrating Life

All books are available at

www.llewellyn.com

Elizabeth Owens, P.O. Box 55, Cassadaga, FL 32706

www.elizabethowens.com

CPSIA information can be obtained
at www.ICGtesting.com
Printed in the USA
FFOW03n0923061215
19331FF